Democracy's Constitution

Democracy's Constitution

Claiming the Privileges of American Citizenship

JOHN DENVIR

UNIVERSITY OF ILLINOIS PRESS

URBANA AND CHICAGO

Library of Congress Cataloging-in-Publication Data
Denvir, John, 1942–
Democracy's constitution: claiming the privileges of
American citizenship / John Denvir.
p.   cm.
Includes index.
ISBN 0-252-02665-9 (cloth: alk. paper)
1. Constitutional law—United States.
2. Civil rights—United States.
3. Political participation—United States.
4. Democracy—United States.
I. Title.
KF4550.D46   2001
342.73'085—dc21   00-012734

For David Rorick,
in thanks for twenty-five years
of good conversation

Contents

Of the People, by the People, and for the People

> That this nation, under God, shall have a new birth of freedom—and that government of the people, by the people, and for the people, shall not perish from the earth.

> —Abraham Lincoln, *The Gettysburg Address*

There are at least three ways to view the U.S. Constitution. As an icon, it is a symbol of American sovereignty that has lasted throughout the country's stormy two-hundred-year history. As a contract, it is a document of dense legal prose. Neither of these views is wrong. The Constitution is an important cultural symbol that in some ways plays for Americans the same role the royal family plays in the United Kingdom. It also is a document with legal consequences for which courts, especially the Supreme Court, often have final say.

But a third view of the Constitution provides the focus for this book. This view sees the Constitution as the blueprint for the American political community. From this perspective, the Constitution sets out the goals of the political enterprise and creates the institutions that can attain them.

The active participation of citizens is pretty much irrelevant to either the icon or the contract view of the Constitution. In fact, too much popular knowledge might undermine the iconic status of a historical document. And ordinary citizens can hardly be expected to master the arcane language in which lawyers transact their business. But if the Constitution is seen as a blueprint for the American political community, all citizens, not just lawyers, must be involved in making it work.

Just as there is more than one way to view the Constitution, there also is more than one "Constitution" to view. First, there is the document hammered out during the hot, sultry summer of 1787 in Philadelphia. This I will call the "first" Constitution. Its primary goals were to bring the thirteen colonies into a political union that would provide the stability necessary for the growth of northern commerce and southern agriculture. But the South exacted a high price for its participation: guarantees for the continuation of slavery. The Constitution's condoning of slavery made it a severely flawed moral document. It also made the political union created by the Constitution a very unstable one, an instability that led ineluctably to four bloody years of civil war.

The North emerged victorious from that war and proceeded to radically change the political structure. Northerners accomplished this by enacting the Thirteenth, Fourteenth, and Fifteenth Amendments, which might be called the "second" Constitution. The Fourteenth Amendment was the primary text of this second Constitution; the intention of the drafters of this amendment was to give constitutional status to two propositions that caused the war after the South rejected them. First, the primary locus of sovereignty would be the national government, not the state governments. Citizens would be Americans first, Virginians or New Yorkers second. Second, every U.S. citizen would enjoy certain rights and privileges that government must respect.

These "privileges or immunities" of U.S. citizenship (as the amendment calls them) are the primary subject of this book. The precise meaning of this oracular phrase is not known. Presumably "privileges" refers to affirmative claims to government action, whereas "immunities" are negative freedoms from government regulation. And while the Fourteenth Amendment does not provide us with a list of the concrete privileges and immunities that are protected, we do know that the drafters intended them to include all those basic civil rights that distinguish a citizen from a slave or a serf. Or, to put it another way, these privileges were to include all those rights that the Declaration of Independence describes as "life, liberty, and the pursuit of happiness."

Most of this book will be an attempt to sketch out what these privileges of American citizenship should look like in the twenty-first century.[1] I argue that they should include the opportunity to earn a living, the right to a first-rate education, the right to a voice that is heard, and the right to a vote that counts. Together with the equal protection clause, the other right for which the Fourteenth Amendment is famous, these rights are the bedrock of my argument.

The list does not sound controversial. At a rhetorical level everyone might agree that every American should enjoy these rights. But a look at how the Constitution operates "on the street" shows a different picture. Few Americans actually enjoy all these rights, and many Americans enjoy none of them in any meaningful sense.

An introductory chapter sets out the basic parameters of this book, focusing primarily on the role of the privileges or immunities clause. Chapter 1 assesses how well current Supreme Court doctrine protects these privileges; my conclusion is that they are not protected at all well. Chapters 2 through 5 then discuss how each privilege should be implemented in the twenty-first century. Chapter 6 does the same for the equal protection clause.

I have been asked several times whether I intend the book for a professional or general audience. The only honest answer I can give is both, because I see my audience as citizens interested in the future of American democracy. Some of these people are lawyers, some not. I recognize that this causes some problems at the outset. Readers without legal training may be reluctant to work with the vocabulary of constitutional law. I hope that I can persuade them that policy discussions in areas like education, free speech, and the vote need the structure of constitutional principle that constitutional theory provides. Still, the book is for the most part free of jargon, and I think the payoff will be worth the effort for the intelligent nonlawyer interested in the future of American democracy.

Lawyers, on the other hand, might at first be impatient with my decision to leaven the analysis of constitutional principles with policy discussions and even anecdotes. I hope that I can convince them that the real world has no airtight division between "law" and "policy." Just as policy discussions need to be disciplined by constitutional principle, constitutional analysis needs to be tested by the concreteness of policy choices. Americans need to jumble the categories of law and policy if society wants a constitution that works in practice as well as theory.

Many readers will disagree with some or all of my policy recommendations. I recognize that when I go beyond the realm of constitutional principle to suggest specific policies in areas like welfare and education, I speak as a citizen rather than an expert. There may be better ways to ensure that all Americans have an opportunity to earn a living and receive a first-class education than the policies I recommend. If so, I would like to hear about them. Good-faith differences of opinion are an essential part of the democratic process.

I do hope, however, that most readers will agree with me on two propositions. The first is that terms like a "first-rate education" and the "opportunity to earn a living" raise issues of constitutional magnitude. By that I mean that citizens can claim them as a matter of constitutional right and need not rely on the goodwill of the legislature. Second, I hope that readers will agree that the resolution of constitutional issues like these should concern all Americans, not only lawyers and judges. I believe that is what Lincoln meant when he declared that democracy is government "of the people, by the people, and for the people."

❖

I would like to give special thanks to three people whose advice has vastly improved this book, Miriam Rokeach, Peter Honigsberg, and John Adler. Another larger group has also helped me by commenting on the text and offering their support: Jeff Brand, john powell, Jackie Caplan-Auerbach, Sarah Caplan, Russell Fong, Alex Auerbach, Michael Denvir, Ken Donnelly, Cathy Bishop, Karen Musalo, Richard

Boswell, Katherine Folger, David and Audrey Fielding, David Rorick, Stephanie Wildman, Pat Mohr, Tom Brown, and Marian and Bill Mogulescu. I would also like to thank Lee Ryan for her help as a research librarian, Laura Mooney and Charles Alfonzo for their research assistance, Kathleen Allenbach for her word-processing skills, and Caren Alpert for her assistance in securing the photographs.

Democracy's Constitution

Introduction   Democracy's Constitution

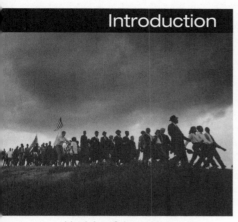

No State shall make or enforce any law which shall abridge the privileges or immunities of citizens of the United States.

—Section 1 of the Fourteenth Amendment

March from Selma to Montgomery.
© James H. Karales. Courtesy of the photographer.

The starting point of this book is the bold statement in the Declaration of Independence that "all men are created equal . . . [and] endowed with certain unalienable rights, that among these are life, liberty, and the pursuit of happiness." Admittedly, the Declaration is an unorthodox place to begin because it was written in 1776 and is not technically part of the Constitution, which was drafted in 1787. But Webster defines *constitution* as "the system or body of fundamental rules and principles of a nation, state, or body politic that determines the powers and duties of the government and guarantees certain rights to the people." Working from that definition, the search for these "fundamental rules and principles" of the American political experience need not be limited to those several paragraphs of flat, legal prose that make up the document written in 1787.

Abraham Lincoln also regarded the Declaration of Independence as the central document of the American political tradition. Because of its status as a national icon, Americans are reluctant to see any flaws in the Constitution; the men and women of Lincoln's generation were genuine in their admiration for it but also willing to note its failures. For Lincoln, the Constitution's greatest flaw was its condoning of slavery, but it had other weaknesses too. The framers had cobbled it together in Philadelphia in an attempt to find a compromise between the interests of southern states and northern states and between small states and large states. It produced some important innovations in political science, like the system of checks and balances between the three departments of the national government. But the states with small populations and the southern states with large slave populations drove a hard bargain before giving their consent to a national union.

The Constitution written in Philadelphia can only be termed *anti-democratic* in many of its provisions. Not only were slaves treated as property but small states received more representation in the Senate than their population warranted, and the southern states got more representation in the House of Representatives than their numbers deserved. The document also incorporated voting qualifications from state law that deprived men without property and all women of the vote.

The 1787 Constitution offered little protection of individual rights, and the rights that were protected were for the most part those of slaveholders and creditors. Additional individual rights were added in the Bill of Rights, which was tacked on in 1791, but, with the important exception of the First Amendment, the Bill of Rights concerned itself mostly with criminal procedure. And the Bill of Rights protected citizens from acts by the national government in an era when state governments were far more important in their everyday lives.

There is little protection for individual rights in the 1787 text. Most of that document is concerned with the nuts and bolts of setting up the new national government. The only hint of protection for "fundamental rights" appears in a vague reference in the Ninth Amendment to other rights "retained by the people," a text the Supreme Court has studiously ignored for two hundred years. But a reason exists for the paucity of rights in the 1787 Constitution. The government structure it ordained left most rights to the jurisdiction of state governments, which remained the primary source of political power. It gave supreme but narrow powers to the national government, mostly in the areas of commerce and foreign policy.

The 1787 Constitution's silence on many of the issues Americans now find so important reflects its acceptance of two key, related ideological beliefs. First, slavery was an accepted practice. Second, citizens owed their primary allegiance to their state government. One was first a Virginian or a New Yorker and only secondarily a citizen of the United States. These assumptions were linked because the slave-holding states believed that only through the acceptance of state autonomy would their investment in human capital be safe.

But those twin assumptions were not to endure. The Civil War was fought over them, and the amendments passed after the North's victory in that most bloody of American wars dramatically altered the structure of American government. The Thirteenth, Fourteenth, and Fifteenth Amendments might fairly be called the Second American Constitution. They also provide the cornerstone for this book.

Studying Abraham Lincoln's Gettysburg Address yields a better idea of how these amendments reshaped the structure of American government. In the address Lincoln sketches the vision of America that the Civil War amendments later attempted to institutionalize. The key contribution of the Gettysburg Address comes from the clarion call of its opening sentence: "Four score and seven years ago our fathers brought forth, upon this continent, a new nation, conceived in liberty, and dedicated to the proposition that 'all men are created equal.'"

This sentence incorporates three important principles. First, "four score and seven" is a direct reference to 1776, and thus to the Declaration, not the Constitution, as the founding document of the American union. Garry Wills points out that "Lincoln distinguished between the Declaration as a statement of a permanent ideal and the Constitution as an early and provisional embodiment of that ideal, to be tested against it, kept in motion toward it."[1] Second, a new "nation" is being birthed, not a confederacy of autonomous states. National sovereignty takes precedence over state autonomy. Third, this nation is dedicated to the revolutionary proposition that "all men are created equal."

The Civil War was fought over these last two propositions. The seceding states denied both; they believed that the primary locus of political sovereignty was found in the individual states, not the national union. They also believed that all men were not created equal; some were born slaves and therefore could be owned by other men. This intellectual dispute ended for all practical purposes with Lee's surrender at Appommattox and was memorialized in the addition to the

Bill of Rights of the Thirteenth, Fourteenth, and Fifteenth Amendments. The people who drafted those amendments believed they were necessary because the Civil War had shown the southern states unwilling to protect the fundamental rights of free men, black or white.[2]

The most important of the three post–Civil War amendments for the purposes of this book is the Fourteenth. It attempted to secure these rights in two separate but related ways. First, section 1 imposes three separate prohibitions on the states to ensure that they do not frustrate the republican vision for post–Civil War America. Then, section 5 of the amendment reserves to Congress the ultimate responsibility to see that the amendment's program is implemented. The first section allows courts to protect citizens against hostile state action, whereas section 5 authorizes Congress to take positive action to implement the amendment's vision.

The first prohibition in section 1 forbids any law that "shall abridge the privileges or immunities of citizens of the United States." The second forbids any state from depriving "any person of life, liberty, or property, without due process of law"; the third prohibits any state to "deny any person within its jurisdiction the equal protection of the laws." While the goal of these prohibitions is the common one of protecting the rights of free men of any color, each plays a specific role. The privileges or immunities clause is substantive; as a member of the American polity, one has certain "perks." The due process clause is grounded in procedure; it requires fair procedures before government acts against the individual. Finally, the equal protection clause focuses on discrimination; it prohibits unjustified differences in treatment.

This book will make good use of all three clauses, but my primary interest is in the privileges or immunities clause. A sad irony is that this clause, which drafters of the Fourteenth Amendment placed first, was gutted soon after its birth by the Supreme Court's opinion in the *Slaughterhouse Cases* (1873).[3] In that case the Court held that the privileges or immunities protected by the amendment included only a narrow list of national rights like access to seaports or the right to government protection while on the high seas. That the drafters of the Fourteenth Amendment would give pride of place to such puny rights defies common sense, and historical scholarship is unanimous in its rejection of the Court's interpretation of the amendment's intent. In fact, more than one hundred years after its error in *Slaughterhouse,* the Supreme Court is beginning to reconsider the constitutional role of the privileges or immunities clause.[4]

But while it is easy to conclude that the Court's interpretation of privileges or immunities was wrong, it is less easy to determine what the amendment does mean by the "privileges or immunities of citizens of the United States." No one agrees on what that imprecise phrase means.[5] Of the two competing theories, one gives the clause "substantive" meaning; it says the clause creates or defines rights that can be enforced by law. The other sees it as requiring only "equality" of treatment, a position that has two major weaknesses. First, the clause speaks in terms of substance—privileges or immunities—not equality. Second, if the privileges or immunities clause is based on equality, there would seem to be little need for the equal protection clause, which the drafters specifically included. The strongest argument for the equality thesis turns out to be a negative one: if the clause were substantive, it would transfer too much power away from the state governments: federal judges would determine what substantive rights qualify as privileges of national citizenship. But, of course, the avowed goal of the Fourteenth Amendment was to make just such a transfer.

The phrase "privileges and immunities" was not a new one. It had already been used in Article IV of the Constitution to protect visitors from neighboring states from discriminatory legislation, for instance, a New York law that said that only residents of New York could engage in the sale of stocks and bonds. Most likely, the drafters of the Fourteenth Amendment were incorporating a definition of privileges and immunities first articulated in the well-known 1823 case of *Corfield v. Coryell:* "those privileges and immunities which are, in their nature, fundamental; which belong, of right, to citizens of all free governments; and which have, at all times, been enjoyed by the citizens of the several states which compose this Union."[6]

In *Corfield* Justice Bushrod Washington was defining the scope of the privileges and immunities clause of Article IV, but his words were very much in the minds of the men who used the same terms in drafting section 1 of the Fourteenth Amendment.

But what "fundamental rights" did the framers of the Fourteenth Amendment have in mind? All scholars agree that the Fourteenth Amendment was intended at least to legitimize the Civil Rights Act of 1866. Certainly, drafters meant to include the rights specifically mentioned in that act, such as the right to make and enforce contracts; to sue and give evidence in court; to inherit, purchase, and sell property. Yet there was no reason for the drafters to use such an expansive phrase as "privileges or immunities" if they meant only to protect this narrow category of rights articulated in the 1866 Civil Rights Act. More likely, as John Hart Ely has pointed out, they intend-

ed the dramatic phrase to set out an abstract ideal that later generations would imbue with more precise content.[7]

Deciding what those privileges of national citizenship should be
in the twenty-first century is the subject of this book. This means
deciding the basic rights each citizen receives when he or she becomes a member of the American national community. If Ely is correct, that the phrase was meant to be an elastic one, there is no reason to limit it to those concrete rights the drafters had in mind. What
counts as a fundamental right may vary by time and place—it would
mean one thing in the primarily rural America of the nineteenth
century and another in the urban postindustrial society of today. As
Justice William Brennan put it: "[T]he ultimate question must be:
What do the words in the text mean in our time? For the genius of
the Constitution rests not in any static meaning it might have had
in a world that is dead and gone, but in the adaptability of its great
principles to cope with current problems and current needs."[8]

Most of the remainder of this book attempts to set out what exactly should be the privileges and immunities of American citizenship as we enter the twenty-first century. I believe the term must be
interpreted to include four privileges: the opportunity to earn a living, the right to a first-rate education, the right to a voice that is
heard, and the right to a vote that counts. This list is not meant to be
exhaustive; for instance, Americans need a national privacy privilege,
and other rights clearly are protected by the Constitution. For instance, in chapter 6, I discuss the special role that the equal protection clause should play. But the four privileges I have listed are central to the goal of ensuring that the Constitution fulfills the promise

of the Declaration of Independence, that all citizens have the opportunity to pursue happiness as they define that term.

First, let us consider the importance of the opportunity to earn a living. Achieving happiness without some financial security is impossible, and the American path to financial security, as I show in chapter 2, is very much tied to productive labor. Some argue that Americans should have a right to housing or a right to medical care; these may be good policy goals, but worthy goals and constitutional rights are different. A constitutional right is a claim against the majority, not a policy one hopes to persuade the majority to adopt. Therefore it must have a firm base in the political tradition. As I explain in chapter 2, I believe the Constitution guarantees American citizens the opportunity to earn a living. Of course, not just any job provides a *living,* a term that I define as employment that produces a paycheck sufficient for housing and medical care.

Second, I argue that the Constitution also extends the right to a first-rate education. This privilege is linked both to the individual's right to earn a living and to her or his role as citizen. Perhaps a strong back was the only prerequisite for productive labor in the nineteenth century, but education is clearly essential to economic success in the twenty-first. And effectively participating in the political system without a good education is impossible. Chapter 3 discusses this right.

The connection between the rights to an opportunity to earn a living and a first-rate education and the goals of the Declaration of Independence are clear. It is difficult to see how a person could achieve happiness without a job or a decent job without a good education. The connection between the right to a voice that is heard and a vote that counts may seem less obvious. These are political rather than social rights and seem less directly related to the pursuit of happiness. But the political system will never create the jobs or fund the schools necessary to fulfill the Declaration's promise without a fundamental reform of U.S. political processes, including the rights of free speech and the vote.

As I argue in chapter 1, neither the opportunity to earn a living nor the right to an education are protected rights under contemporary U.S. constitutional law. This book breaks new ground in embracing them. But the other two privileges—the rights to effective speech and to a meaningful vote—are protected, at least in a diluted form. Freedom of speech has been ruled a liberty protected by the due process clause of the Fourteenth Amendment, and the right to vote has been ruled a fundamental right under the equal protection clause of the Fourteenth Amendment. One could quibble that the Court has misused the due process and equal protection clauses to perform tasks intended for the privileges or immunities clause, but my disagreement with the Court is more substantial than that. I point out in chapter 1 that the Court has recognized speech and the vote as fundamental but construes those rights so narrowly as to undermine their value to most citizens. So, as chapters 4 and 5 discuss, the question for this book is not whether speech and the vote are fundamental rights enjoyed by all citizens but what those rights will mean in the twenty-first century. I would go beyond the current minimal protections of the rights to free speech and the vote to the more ambitious goal of ensuring every citizen a voice that is heard and a vote that counts.

The book's main concern is the privileges or immunities clause, but I also will discuss the equal protection clause, in chapter 6. The equal protection clause complements the role of the privileges or immunities clause. The privileges or immunities clause protects claims to affirmative government action (privileges) and claims to protection from government action (immunities); each is substantive. The equal protection clause looks not at substance but at differences in treatment, especially differences based on race. It asks whether differences in treatment between groups can be justified as necessary to achieve some common goal.

In equal protection, as in privileges or immunities, the benchmark that the amendment uses is the condemnation of slavery. Just as the privileges and immunities of American citizenship are those that distinguish a free person from a slave, so too the model for equal protection of the laws is whether the government action has treated all citizens, but especially racial minorities, as civic equals. Martin Luther King's "I Have a Dream Speech" provides inspiration for considering the contemporary content of the equal protection clause: "[W]e will be able to speed up that day when *all* God's children, black men and white men, Jews and Gentiles, Protestants, and Catholics, will be able to join hands and sing in the words of the old Negro spiritual, 'Free at last! Free at last! Thank God Almighty, we are free at last!'"[9]

The privileges or immunities clause and the equal protection clause are both wellsprings of judicial power. As I recount in chapter 1, the Supreme Court has failed to vigorously enforce these clauses. Case law needs to be overturned. But this book is not a Court-centered enterprise. Fundamental rights go beyond what courts can enforce by decree. And protecting them also requires affirmative legislative action. This is clearly true in regard to ensuring that every American has a first-rate education and the opportunity to earn a living. I will show that it is also true with regard to a voice that is heard and a vote that counts. Much of what I describe in this book requires legislative action. Fortunately, section 5 of the Fourteenth Amendment also gives Congress ample power to enforce the requirements of the amendment. This congressional power, together with the spending power set forth in Article I, gives Congress broad power to create and fund the institutions that will make a reality of the reforms that I advocate.

But before I describe this program, I will survey how well the Supreme Court today protects the rights of U.S. citizens.

The 1939 Hughes Court. Photograph by Harris & Ewing. Reproduced from the Collection of the Supreme Court of the United States.

1 Too Important to Leave to Judges

War is much too serious a matter to be entrusted to the military.

—French proverb

Before I address the future of the privileges or immunities clause, I should pause to assess how well constitutional law has done without it. As I pointed out in the introduction, the Supreme Court squelched the privileges or immunities clause in the *Slaughterhouse Cases* in 1873. Here I discuss the current state of the law in those areas most central to my thesis—the opportunity to earn a living, obtain a first-rate education, exercise free speech and the vote, and be afforded equal protection. After twenty-five years of teaching constitutional law, I have come to believe that Americans vastly overestimate the constitutional rights they actually possess; certainly, this is true in the areas under discussion.

One conclusion I hope readers will draw from the case histories in this chapter is the need to resurrect the privileges or immunities clause. But a second and related point is whether citizens should accept the current interpretations of the Supreme Court or make their own decisions about the meaning of the Constitution. I don't mean whether or not citizens should engage in civil disobedience, but whether American society should accord Supreme Court decisions moral authority beyond their legal status. Most Americans associate the Constitution with the Supreme Court. That is only natural because the Supreme Court has played an extremely important role in the Constitution's history. But Americans have a tendency to go even further, to equate the Constitution with the current Supreme Court's interpretation of it. This is a grave error, as I hope the story of the case of *Plessy v. Ferguson* will illustrate.[1]

In 1894 Homer Plessy, a man of mixed race, purchased a first-class rail ticket in New Orleans for a trip to a nearby town. He took his place in the first-class carriage, only to be told by the conductor that he would have to ride in the car assigned to the "colored race." When Plessy refused to move, he was forcibly ejected from the train and imprisoned in the New Orleans jail. He was charged with violating a Louisiana statute that required that passengers ride in the carriages assigned to members of their race. He challenged the statute as a violation of his rights under the Fourteenth Amendment's equal protection clause, a challenge that eventually found its way to the U.S. Supreme Court.

The Court quickly rejected Plessy's suit. Justice Henry Brown spoke for the Court in an opinion that only thinly veiled his hostility toward Plessy's claim. First, Brown trivialized the goal of the Fourteenth Amendment by gratuitously assuming "in the nature of things it [the Amendment] could not have been intended to abolish distinctions based upon color, or to enforce social, as distinguished from political equality, or a commingling of the two races upon terms unsatisfactory to either." Brown then proceeded to ridicule Plessy's argument that state-supported racial segregation "stamps the colored race with a badge of inferiority." "If this be so," Brown noted, "it is not by reason of anything found in the Act, but solely because the colored race chooses to put that construction upon it."[2]

Brown then concluded his discussion with a short lecture on the dangers of attempting to control "racial instincts": "If the two races are to meet on terms of social equality, it must be the result of natural affinities, a mutual appreciation of each other's merits and a voluntary consent of individuals. . . . Legislation is powerless to eradicate racial instincts or to abolish distinctions based upon racial differences, and the attempt to do so can only result in accentuating the difficulties of the present situation."[3]

The Supreme Court's decision in *Plessy* was widely accepted as applying to situations well beyond the segregation of railway carriages to validate an American-style apartheid in all areas of life in the South. It was only necessary that the facilities afforded African Americans were in theory "separate but equal." In fact, they could be and were always separate but never equal.

With the benefit of the hindsight of history, three things about *Plessy* are clear. It was legally wrong when decided. It was later overturned in the Supreme Court's 1954 landmark decision in *Brown v. Board of Education*.[4] And it was overturned because a group of citizens refused to accept the Supreme Court's interpretation of the Four-teenth Amendment and engaged in a long, arduous, and ultimately successful struggle to have the Court correct its error.[5]

The experience of *Plessy* should convince Americans that consti-tutional law is too important to leave to the judges. Citizens must always respect the legal efficacy of a Supreme Court decision, but, like those who refused to accept *Plessy,* whether the Supreme Court has made a proper interpretation of the Constitution is a decision each citizen must make. And *Plessy* and the *Slaughterhouse Cases* are not the only time the Supreme Court has erred. The infamous 1857 *Dred Scott* decision held that slaves were property, not people, for purposes of constitutional law.[6]

To evaluate the current Supreme Court's performance in the ar-eas of law in which I am most interested, I have chosen the method of positing one case as representative of the Court's performance in a specific area. I acknowledge that I have not chosen these cases ran-domly, but I do believe that they are representative of the Court's record as a whole.

The Opportunity to Earn a Living

The 1979 case of *New York City Transit Authority v. Beazer* is a good example of the Court's approach to a citizen's right to gainful em-ployment.[7] Carl Beazer was a forty-year-old African American who was fired after working for ten years cleaning out subway cars for the New York City Transit Authority. Beazer had been a heroin addict for almost all those years, but he was not fired for using heroin; he was fired for using methadone, which was prescribed for him in the drug addiction recovery program he entered to kick his habit. He was fired for getting help.

Methadone is a narcotic that is substituted for heroin in treatment because it prevents withdrawal symptoms such as a craving for drugs but provides no high, or euphoric feelings. But, to the bureaucratic mind of the New York City Transit Authority, a narcotic is a narcotic and therefore Beazer fell under its rule forbidding narcotic use by employees.

Beazer brought his constitutional claim under the equal protection clause because the privileges or immunities clause had been rendered impotent by the *Slaughterhouse Cases.* The first thing to remember about the equal protection clause is that it does not protect substantive rights like free speech; instead, it guards against improper differences in treatment. For instance, an eight-year-old-child who tells his parents that he has a right to stay up until 9 o'clock makes a "substantive rights" argument—he is saying he has an inherent right to do so. If he argues instead that he should be allowed to stay up till 9 o'clock because his older sister did when she was eight, he is now making an "equal protection" argument—you cannot treat people who are similarly situated (eight years old) differently without justifying the difference in treatment.

The second thing to remember about equal protection is that the Court does not always require the government to justify the difference in treatment in the same way. Often it will presume that government had a good reason for treating people differently and will not require much justification. For instance, the government may not have many good reasons for limiting highway speed to 55 miles per hour instead of 65 miles per hour. The difference in safety and gas economy may be minimal when compared to the inconvenience and economic inefficiency. But if a motorist arrested for going 60 miles per hour in 55-mile-per-hour zone were to argue that his equal protection rights were violated because he was treated differently than a motorist driving 55 miles per hour, he will lose. Even if he could show that driving 60 miles per hour is no more dangerous than 55 miles per hour, the Court would not care to second-guess the legislature on what speed is too fast, so long as the legislature's judgment was rational. But sometimes the Court will insist on a stronger justification for a difference in treatment. When a rational explanation is not enough, the Court will engage in "strict scrutiny," asking the government to show that the treatment was the only effective way to attain an important government goal.

One situation in which strict scrutiny will be applied is when the government uses a suspect classification like race or nationality. For instance, if the transit authority used the regulation to terminate only African Americans or Puerto Ricans who used methadone, the Court would require a strong reason to justify the regulation. Of course, as I will discuss later, governments today never write such overtly discriminatory regulations. Another situation in which strict scrutiny will be invoked is when the regulation affects a "fundamental right." As I show in chapter 2, there is a strong argument that the opportunity to earn a living is such a fundamental right, but the modern Supreme Court has refused to recognize it as such. Therefore Beazer and his colleagues had to use the "rational basis" test, a lesser standard of equal protection, in arguing their case.

At first, this did not appear to be an insuperable obstacle because a regulation that leads the agency to fire workers for trying to get help does not seem to be a very rational way to run a subway system. At trial Beazer's lawyers introduced exhaustive evidence, all of which showed that methadone does not affect job performance and that many former drug users have returned to productive lives by using methadone for a transitional period. In fact, the trial court found as a factual matter that, after a year of successful treatment with methadone, former drug users were just as likely to be good employees as members of the general population and, furthermore, that monitoring methadone users to make sure they did not use drugs or alcohol could be done efficiently through the transit authority's normal employment procedures. In other words, because former drug users with a year of methadone treatment were just as likely to be good employees as other workers, a blanket rule denying them work violated the equal protection clause. If they were just as likely as other employees to do a good job, singling them out for termination merely because they took methadone was discriminatory. The trial court ruled for Beazer.

The Supreme Court overruled the trial court and in its opinion strove mightily to find some rational justification for the transit authority's rule. The Court argued that the policy was rational because "any special rule short of total exclusion that the [transit authority] might adopt is likely to be less precise—and will assuredly be more costly than the one that it currently enforces."[8]

But, as a dissenting justice pointed out, this simply was not true. A rule that selects out only methadone users who are statistically an employment risk (those with less than a year of treatment) is more, not less, precise than one that requires the firing of all methadone users, including those who are likely to make good employees. And because the transit authority already had procedures for checking up on employees, it would incur no added costs by applying those procedures for ensuring that methadone users were continuing their treatment.

The Court's ruling was unaffected by evidence showing that the transit authority's hard-line approach to people attempting to kick heroin was inconsistent with its quite flexible policies for employees recovering from alcoholism. The decision also ignored evidence that approximately 65 percent of the participants in methadone-based drug recovery programs were African Americans and Latinos, members of groups whose history of discrimination gives them special claim on the equal protection clause. Is the Court's decision fair to Carl Beazer or even to the taxpayers who will have to support Beazer if he is not allowed to work?

In chapter 2, I examine how the privileges or immunities clause might change the life of Carl Beazer and millions of other American workers.

A First-Rate Education

In *Savage Inequalities,* education expert Jonathan Kozol gives us a harrowing sketch of the school experience of poor children at East St. Louis High School, which he visited in 1990. He started his tour at the machine shop, which he found unused for lack of staff; the school district had recently laid off 286 teachers and twenty-six aides because of budget cuts. When Kozol noted that the fifteen students in an introductory home economics class were sitting at their desks doing nothing, the teacher explained that Friday was "cleanup" day and students do no work on that day. He then asked whether the course provided job training; the teacher said that only advanced home economics offered such training. To his final inquiry about the type of job students trained in "advanced home economics" might land, the answer was "fast food places—Burger King, McDonald's."

Kozol's tour continued into the physics lab, which was woefully unequipped. The water pipes had been taken out. The physics teacher commented wistfully, "It would be great if we had water." The chemistry lab was fairly well equipped, but the chemistry teacher informed him that it could not be used because he had thirty students in the class and one teacher could safely supervise no more than twenty in the lab.

Kozol then visited the history department, where the teacher commented that all he had to work with was the one assigned textbook; the school didn't even own a VCR. Indeed, the lack of resources was not limited to academic courses; the football field had no crossbars for the goalposts.[9]

Is it surprising to learn that only 55 percent of the entering class at East St. Louis High graduates and only 10 percent go on to four-year colleges? What other result would one expect? And while the deplorable conditions at East St. Louis High have many causes, one is the Supreme Court's 1973 decision in *San Antonio v. Rodriguez* in which the Court endorsed state systems of school financing that enable rich suburbs to operate sophisticated college preparatory academies while poor districts like East St. Louis are still hoping for a VCR and crossbars for the goalposts.[10]

The case involved the Texas system of school financing, but the Court's decision had repercussions well beyond the Lone Star State.

The case involved a claim by Mexican-American students that Texas had deprived them of equal protection of the laws by instituting a system of school financing that yielded for their schools about half as many dollars per student as were spent on students attending affluent suburban public schools in the same county. The Texas scheme, like that of most states, relied heavily on the local property tax to produce school district revenues. This meant that a district with high property values could raise a lot of money, but a district with low property values could not. For example, the complicated Texas scheme raised only $356 for the education of each student in the inner-city Edgewood school district, whereas it raised $594 for each student educated in the affluent suburban Alamo Heights School District. This inequality existed even though the voters in Edgewood voted to tax their property, the main source of school revenues, at a higher rate than property was taxed in Alamo Heights.

In human terms it meant that students in the Edgewood district were, as Justice Thurgood Marshall pointed out in his dissent, "forced to attend an underfunded school with poorer physical facilities, less experienced teachers, larger classes and a narrower range of courses."[11] In other words, their education was more like that of students in faraway East St. Louis than nearby Alamo Heights.

As I noted earlier, one situation in which the Court will invoke strict scrutiny is when the difference in treatment relates to a fundamental right. The plaintiffs whose children attended the poorly funded schools in the Edgewood district had hoped that the Court would subject the Texas scheme to strict scrutiny review on the ground that education is a fundamental right. This seemed a reasonable hope because in *Brown v. Board of Education,* the Court called education "perhaps the most important function of state and local governments."[12] But in *Rodriguez* the Supreme Court made one of those distinctions for which lawyers are notorious: "[T]he importance of a service performed by the State does not determine whether it must be regarded as fundamental for purposes of examination under the Equal Protection Clause."[13] One might ask why not.

Faced with the Court's refusal to require an extremely persuasive justification for the lopsided Texas education-financing scheme, the plaintiffs (like Carl Beazer) were forced to argue that the scheme could not be justified as a rational legislative judgment. Texas attempted to counter that claim by saying that its school-financing scheme was intended to maximize local control of educational quality by individual districts. In other words, districts that wanted high-quality schools could tax themselves heavily; those that wanted lower property taxes would accept less expensive schools. But the lawyers for the poor children pointed out that the Texas system did not achieve the desired goal of local control for all districts. Some districts with a lot of high-priced properties on the tax rolls, like Alamo Heights, could choose between expensive schools and a low tax rate, but poor districts like Edgewood had no such choice. No matter how high the rate at which they taxed themselves, the low property values in their districts would mean that voters could never raise enough money to provide a high quality education for their children.

The Court did not disagree with the factual premise; it merely dismissed its legal significance: "While it is no doubt true that reliance on local property taxation for school revenues provides less freedom of choice with respect to expenditures for some districts than others, the existence of some inequality in the manner in which the

State's rationale is achieved is not alone a sufficient basis for striking down the entire system."[14] But the plaintiffs were not asking the Court to "strike down the entire" Texas system; they were asking that its operation be reformed so that all students had a chance at a good education. In chapter 3, I examine how schooling in San Antonio and East St. Louis might change if a "first-rate education" were a privilege of American citizenship.

A Voice That Is Heard

Clark v. Community for Creative Non-violence (1984) is a good example of the Court's current approach to free speech.[15] No one would doubt that freedom of speech is a fundamental right; the U.S. Constitution is revered all over the world for its ringing defense of speech. Yet often a right respected at the level of theory is not well protected at the level of practice. The *Clark* case is a good example. In 1982, when widespread homelessness was not yet a well-known aspect of urban life in the United States, a nonprofit group sought permission to set up a temporary "tent city" in Lafayette Park, which is opposite the White House, to dramatize the plight of the homeless during the freezing winter months. The group won permission to set up temporary tents and to keep a vigil in the tents day and night, but the National Park Service denied the organization permission to have demonstrators sleep in the tents to dramatize the suffering of the homeless on cold winter nights all over the country. The park service said that while "feigned sleeping" was permissible, actual dozing off would constitute "camping," a violation of park regulations.

The Court conceded that sleeping in this context was speech and therefore protected but pointed out that the "no-camping" regulation was not aimed at the message of the demonstration and therefore was less threatening to protesters' First Amendment rights. The Court reasoned that the park service's goal was to protect the grass and shrubbery, and refusing permission for sleeping in the tents was an appropriate way to achieve that goal. Even though the Court had no reason to believe that real sleeping did any more damage to the grass than the feigned sleeping that was allowed, it still ruled for the park service, claiming that the First Amendment gave the judiciary no "authority to replace the Park Service as the manager of the Nation's parks or endow the judiciary with the competence to judge how much protection of park lands is wise."[16]

Once the Court was satisfied that the government's motive was not disagreement with the message of a demonstration about homelessness, the free speech dimension of the case disappeared. The Court refused to second-guess the National Park Service regarding how much wear and tear on the park was too much. Of course, this refusal meant that the bureaucracy had the final say on the free speech rights of the demonstrators. That is a question that the Constitution allocates to the courts.

The Court's decision deprived the protesters of their right to effective speech. The demonstration was their best chance to affect public policy. Unlike wealthy groups, they could not buy television time to get their message across. They could only create an event that would attract press and television coverage. In this day and age television demands powerful "visuals"; for television producers the difference between real sleeping and feigned sleeping is obvious. The morning news wants to see sleepy people with big yawns scratching their bellies as they line up for their oatmeal. As it did in *Rodriguez,* and in *Beazer,* the Court failed to weigh the government's explanation against the effect its decisions had on the constitutional rights of citizens; instead, it accepted the government's own balance. The result was that the protesters were unnecessarily deprived of what I call a voice that is heard. In chapter 4, I discuss how the constitutional right to free speech might look if the privileges or immunities clause were interpreted as insisting that all citizens have a voice that is heard.

A Vote That Counts

City of Mobile v. Bolden (1984) will serve as my exemplar of the Court's protection of a meaningful vote.[17] The right to vote is another of those rights that is better protected in theory than in practice. The Supreme Court is fond of pointing out that the vote is fundamental because it is "preservative of other basic civil and political rights."[18] The point is an important one. After all, if the minority parents in *Rodriguez* had wielded more political power in the Texas legislature, they would not have needed to file suit.

Unfortunately, most Americans do not have an effective vote. Wiley Bolden is an example. Bolden was an African American who lived in Mobile, Alabama, in the 1970s. He regularly voted in elections for the important office of city commissioner. Yet his candidates never won. For Bolden the vote was pure ritual; it gave him no power. Like most Americans, Bolden usually voted for candidates of the same race as he. In the 1970s African Americans comprised 35 percent of the population of Mobile, so one would have expected that approximately one-third of the commissioners elected would be African American. In fact, not one African-American candidate was elected to the Mobile city commission in the twentieth century.

Race certainly played a role in this scandalous situation, but it was not the only causal factor. Even if one assumes that whites would not vote for African-American candidates, one would still expect an African American to win sometimes. But whites were able to avoid this result by adopting an "at-large" form of elections in Mobile. This means that rather than splitting the city into three (or five or seven) districts, each of which would elect one commissioner, Mobile chose to allow all voters throughout the city to vote for all three commissioner positions. At-large elections permit the majority to swamp minorities in a larger sea of opposing votes. For instance, because Mobile was racially segregated in its housing patterns, a vote by district should have enabled African Americans to elect an African-American commissioner. But because the elections were citywide, African Americans were always outvoted 65 percent to 35 percent for all three commissioner positions.

It is important to recognize that the African Americans of Mobile suffered more than a symbolic injury by not being able to elect even one city commissioner. Their political impotence deprived them of almost any role in local government and any share of the patronage that comes from supporting successful candidates. For instance, the city had several committees of citizens appointed by the commissioners. Predictably, these appointees seldom were African Americans. Political influence also leads to city jobs, which may explain why only fifteen of 435 Mobile fire fighters were black and why the police force was also segregated. The story with city services was the same; streets in black areas were less likely to be paved, and even the golf course sup-

ported by tax monies was open only to whites. Mobile's commissioners even used city taxes to defend this segregation in court.[19]

The Supreme Court upheld the at-large election system in Mobile. It held that Bolden's rights had not been violated because the
equal protection clause prohibits only "purposeful" racial discrimination and the Court had insufficient proof that Mobile's choice of
the at-large system had been adopted for the purpose of harming
blacks. As I show in chapter 6, the Court was wrong on that point;
minorities should not be required to show an evil "purpose" in order
to bring a claim of race discrimination. But Mobile had violated another of Bolden's fundamental rights, one the Court completely ignored. The city had deprived him of a vote that counts. This is an
injury he shares with most Americans, white as well as black.

The African Americans in Mobile were the victim of a gerrymander, a scheme to rig elections to favor one side. The strong suspicion,
of course, is that African Americans were the victims of a racially discriminatory gerrymander and that racial prejudice influenced the
Mobile decision to use at-large voting. But the gerrymander was also
political because blacks in Mobile also constituted a political minority. In fact, Republicans would have fared no better. If Republicans
had made up 35 percent of the electorate in Mobile, they too would
have found themselves consistently losing 65 percent to 35 percent,
and they too would have been fenced out of all the perks of municipal government.

At-large elections are just one form of gerrymandering. Another
popular tactic is to draw the boundaries of election districts to maximize the majority party's voting strength. Gerrymanders can even
be bipartisan, as when both parties agree to draw districts to create

safe seats for their incumbents. Experts say that any election in which the winning margin is more than 10 percent is not competitive, so one side or the other had a safe seat before the campaign even began. In the elections for the legislative assembly in New York State in 1996, 201 of the 211 seats were won by margins of more than 10 percent, a result that the *New York Times* attributed to gerrymandering by the major parties. Fewer than 5 percent of the election districts saw true democratic competition. As the *Times* commented, New Yorkers "have no more voting options than North Koreans."[20] This may be politics, but it is certainly not democracy. If the New York pattern prevails throughout the United States (and experts say it does), most Americans share the same political impotence.

The Supreme Court has accepted gerrymanders as part of the American political system. Racial gerrymanders are not in violation of the Constitution unless the complainant can meet the demanding level of proof required by *Mobile v. Bolden*. Gerrymanders to maximize one party's power are even more likely to withstand attack.[21] And while the loss of an effective vote is a less tangible injury than the loss of a job or being forced to attend a rundown school, it results in a political impotence that causes the more concrete injuries like the segregated police force that African Americans in Mobile experienced. In chapter 5, I examine how all this might change if Americans insist on a vote the counts.

The Equal Protection of the Laws

McCleskey v. Kemp (1987) is a good example of the Court's approach to claims of racial discrimination under the equal protection clause of the Fourteenth Amendment.[22] Warren McCleskey was charged with killing a white police officer who interrupted him during the commission of a robbery in Georgia. McCleskey denied he had shot the officer, but ballistics tests connected the gun in McCleskey's possession to one of the two bullets in the officer's body. The local district attorney asked for the death penalty. McCleskey was duly tried, convicted, and sentenced to death.

McCleskey filed a lawsuit alleging that both the prosecutor's decision to ask for the death penalty and the jury's decision to order it were unconstitutionally tainted by racial prejudice in violation of the Fourteenth Amendment's equal protection clause. To support his claim McCleskey submitted what the Supreme Court conceded was a sophisticated statistical study that demonstrated that race was an important factor in the death penalty process in Georgia. Black defendants not only were more likely to receive the death penalty than white defendants but defendants of any race were more likely to die if they killed whites than if they killed blacks. Prosecutors and jurors evidently put a lesser value on the life of an African-American victim. McCleskey was on the wrong side of the numbers on both issues; he was a black who had killed a white. This made his chances of receiving the death penalty in Georgia seven times greater than if he had been a white who killed a black.[23]

It is important to understand what McCleskey was asking the Court to do. If the Georgia legislature had passed a statute that explicitly stated that whites who murder whites would be given life sentences while blacks who murdered whites would receive the death penalty, the statute would clearly be unconstitutional as a violation of equal protection of the laws. But the statute did not speak in racial terms; McCleskey's argument was that it was administered on a racial basis, that because of conscious or unconscious racism prosecutors were much more likely to ask for the death penalty in cases with black defendants and that juries were much more likely to vote the death penalty against black defendants.

McCleskey's lawyers did not claim that his sentence should be reversed on the basis of a statistical study; they conceded reasons other than racial prejudice might explain the statistics. They claimed that the study raised enough doubt about the fairness of the system under which McCleskey was sentenced to require Georgia to come forward with some persuasive nonracial explanation for the damning statistics.

Justice Lewis Powell wrote the majority opinion. He did not challenge the conclusions of McCleskey's studies but refused to require Georgia to defend its system against the charge of racism. His opinion is not a very persuasive document in any of its arguments.[24] But one of his reasons for refusing to require Georgia to defend its administration of the death penalty illustrates especially well the thesis that constitutional law is too important to leave to the judges: "[I]f we accepted McCleskey's claim that racial bias has impermissibly tainted the capital sentencing decision, we could soon be faced with similar claims as to other types of penalty."[25] In other words, if the Court admitted the possibility of racial prejudice in McCleskey's trial, it might have to face up to the possibility of racial prejudice in thousands of other decisions by prosecutors and juries. Powell argued that it would be so embarrassing to face up to the existence of racism in the justice system that it is more prudent to allow Warren McCleskey to die. As Justice William Brennan said wryly in dissent, this argument is based on "a fear of too much justice."[26] It also gives a whole new twist to the old saying that Justice is blind.

In chapter 6, I discuss how the Court ought to reinterpret the equal protection clause to remedy the injustice done in the *McCleskey* case, and I examine how race should and should not be used to affirmatively remedy the effects of racial discrimination.

I hope this short survey has made the case that Americans' constitutional rights in the areas of an opportunity to earn a living, obtain an education, and exercise free speech and the vote range from nonexistent to narrow and that the equal protection clause is not performing its proper role of protecting minorities. Americans should certainly urge on courts a more generous interpretation of both the privileges or immunities clause and the equal protection clause.

But constitutional law is too important to leave to the judges for another reason. Even if judges were to make the correct interpretation, the constitutional rights I have outlined would not necessarily become a reality; full enjoyment of these rights requires legislative action beyond the authority of the courts. These rights need to be supported by generous funding in order to be implemented effectively, and courts have no power to authorize such expenditures. For that reason this book is a blueprint for legislative action as well as a judicial analysis.

2 The Opportunity to Earn a Living

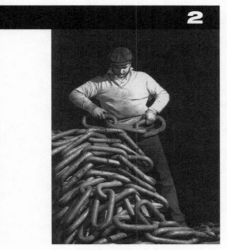

A steelworker making chains for ships and industry. Courtesy of Tony Stone Images/Chicago Inc.

The privileges and immunities designated are those which of right belong to citizens of all free governments. Clearly among these must be the right to pursue a lawful employment in a lawful manner, without other restraint than such as equally affects all persons.

—Justice Stephen J. Field, dissenting in the *Slaughterhouse Cases*

Work has always been an essential component of the American Dream. John Smith had barely landed at Jamestown in 1607 when he declared that in America "every man may be master and owner of his own labour and land."[1] As a nineteenth-century French tourist, Michel Chevalier, put it, life in America is "delightful in the eyes of him who prefers work to every thing else, and with whom work can take the place of every thing else."[2] For Americans work is not only necessary for economic independence, it also defines our status; in fact, Judith Sklar argues that work is at the core of citizenship—"a citizen is neither an aristocrat or a slave, but an economically productive and independent agent."[3]

In a work-obsessed society the inability to earn a living is more than a source of physical deprivation, it becomes a form of public humiliation, a sign of personal worthlessness. Remember the plight of the Joad family in John Steinbeck's *The Grapes of Wrath*? Natural disaster had forced the Joads off the family farm in Oklahoma's dust bowl of the thirties, depriving them of the means of earning a living. The physical deprivation was terrible, but the spiritual blow to their dignity was even worse. As Sklar puts it, "We are citizens only if we earn."[4]

"Free labor" was a core doctrine of the Republican Party in the 1850s and 1860s, and it was the Republicans who controlled the drafting of the Fourteenth Amendment, including the privileges or immunities clause. The opportunity for social advancement through labor was to Republican minds the factor that distinguished the United States (at least the North) from Europe: "What is it that makes the great mass of American citizens so much more enterprising and intelligent than the laboring classes in Europe? It is the stimulant held out to them by the character of our institutions. The door is thrown open to all, and even the poorest and humblest in the land, may, by industry and application, attain a position which will entitle him to the respect and confidence of his fellow-men."[5]

The Republicans' primary goal during Reconstruction was to enable the freed slave to share in this vision of free labor, to attain an independent base of property, which signified full citizenship.[6] This is reflected in the text of the Civil Rights Act of 1866, which gave federal protection to the rights of ex-slaves to contract, own property, and sue. Through protecting former slaves' right to contract for a fair wage, the Republicans planned to secure former slaves' independence. Meanwhile, former slaveholders hoped to keep former slaves in virtual bondage by limiting these "civil rights."[7] The desire to quiet any doubts about the constitutionality of that Civil Rights Act of 1866 was the catalyst for the drafting of the Fourteenth Amendment. But the amendment does not speak in terms of race; it was meant to protect all Americans in their fundamental rights as citizens.

One would think that these fundamental rights would include the opportunity to earn a living. The right to pursue one's livelihood has always been considered one of the fundamental rights protected by the privileges and immunities clause of Article IV.[8] Why would the phrase not bear the same meaning in the Fourteenth Amendment? In Article IV the clause has only limited application because it has been interpreted to require only that states not discriminate against citizens from neighboring states. But if the right to earn a living were a privilege of American citizenship protected by the Fourteenth Amendment, it would give substantive protection to all American workers whose livelihood was threatened by government action.

Soon after ratification of the Fourteenth Amendment, workers argued that the privileges or immunities clause did just that. The controversy before the Supreme Court has become known as the *Slaughterhouse Cases* (1873).[9] The City of New Orleans had given one group of butchers a monopoly on slaughtering animals in the city. Another group of butchers, put out of business by the ordinance, sued, claiming that prohibiting the practice of their profession deprived them of one of the privileges or immunities of citizenship protected by section 1.

Justice Joseph P. Bradley readily agreed: "[T]he right of any citizen to follow whatever lawful employment he chooses to adopt (submitting himself to all lawful regulations) is one of his most valuable

rights, and one which the legislature . . . cannot invade."[10] Justice
Stephen J. Field agreed with Bradley, even connecting the history of
the text of the Reconstruction amendments with the free labor ideology: "The abolition of slavery and involuntary servitude was intended to make everyone born in this country a free man, and as such
to give him the right to pursue the ordinary avocations of life without other restraint than such as affects all others, and to enjoy equally
with them the fruits of his labor."[11]

Unfortunately, Bradley and Field were writing in dissent; the
Court ruled 5-4 against the New Orleans butchers, reading the privileges or immunities clause so narrowly that the phrase disappeared
as a functional part of the Constitution for more than 125 years. But
while this book must recognize the decision in the *Slaughterhouse
Cases* as legal precedent, citizens need not accept it as a proper interpretation of the Constitution. My dissenting view joins the long list
of those scholars who have studied the question and concluded that
the *Slaughterhouse Cases* were wrongly decided.[12] The Supreme Court
now appears to agree. In 1999 the Court used the privileges or immunities clause to strike down a California welfare law.[13] The Court's
opinion was analytically slippery, but it does open the door to recon-
sidering the status of the clause, and Americans can hope that the
Court will eventually return the privileges or immunities clause to its
rightful place as the primary source of protection for fundamental
rights of U.S. citizenship. But even if the Court refuses to abandon its
narrow reading of the privileges or immunities clause, the clause itself is still an integral part of the Constitution and voters can demand
that Congress implement it.

The Supreme Court may have crippled the privileges or immunities clause, but the free labor ideology behind it survived to reassert itself in another guise. After *Slaughterhouse* the privileges or immunities clause itself fell into disuse, but the Court "discovered" remarkably similar content in another clause of section 1 of the Fourteenth Amendment, the due process clause. The original intent of the due process clause was primarily to provide for fair procedures when government infringed upon "life, liberty, or property," but the Supreme Court soon decided that the word *liberty* also protected certain substantive rights. Here is how in 1897 the Supreme Court defined *liberty* in *Allgeyer v. Louisiana:* "The liberty mentioned . . . means not only the right of the citizen to be free from the mere physical restraint of his person . . . but is deemed to embrace the right of the citizen to be free in the employment of all his faculties; to be free to use them in all lawful ways; to live and work where he will; *to earn his livelihood by a lawful calling;* to pursue any livelihood or avocation, and for that purpose to enter into all contracts which may be proper."[14] This, of course, sounds very much like the argument about the privileges or immunities clause that the butchers had made unsuccessfully in the *Slaughterhouse Cases* twenty-four years earlier.

Matters came to a head in 1905 in the famous Supreme Court case of *Lochner v. New York.*[15] *Lochner* involved a Progressive-era New York labor law that restricted the number of hours a baker could work to ten hours a day and sixty hours a week. Capitalists were outraged by such "socialist" legislation, which they believed upset the "eternal laws" of laissez-faire economics. In the *Lochner* decision the justices were able to twist the Fourteenth Amendment's free labor ideology to capitalist ends. The majority of the Court ruled that the statutory limitation on the hours a baker could work violated his "liberty of contract" to work more than ten hours a day or sixty hours a week.

Because the law involved in *Lochner* is now considered a rather uncontroversial wages-and-hours measure necessary in an industrial economy, the Court's result in *Lochner* is universally condemned. The orthodox view now holds that the Court's error in *Lochner* was to hold that the Constitution protects economic or social rights in any form, and therefore legislatures should have a free rein in the area of economic and social policy. This extreme reaction to *Lochner* leads to the ironic conclusion that the Constitution protects least that which citizens value most—their ability to earn a living.

Citizens can disapprove of the holding in *Lochner* without abandoning the free labor ideology behind the Fourteenth Amendment. The right to earn a living (or the liberty to contract) is not an absolute right. As Justices Field and Bradley pointed out in their dissents in the *Slaughterhouse Cases,* this right is subject to reasonable regulation in the public interest. The mistake that the majority made in *Lochner* was not recognizing that legislation to prevent employers from coercing bakers into working long hours for low wages was a reasonable regulation of the liberty of contract. That the right to earn a living is a fundamental right does not mean that a worker can never be fired; it just means the firing must be justified. Neither does it mean that legislatures cannot intervene to protect workers' rights by means of reasonable regulations.

Despite the questionable validity of the Court's holding in *Lochner,* it is important to remember that "substantive due process" (as the *Lochner* doctrine came to be known) was not always used to harm workers. A good example is the post–World War I case of *Meyer v. Nebraska.*[16] During and after World War I, the United States suffered a virulent attack of xenophobia. German Americans were a natural target. Nebraska passed a law making it a crime to teach German to young children. Meyer, a German teacher by profession, challenged the law, and the Supreme Court ruled in his favor, once again relying on an interpretation of the word *liberty* that sounded very much like content ascribed to the privileges or immunities clause: "Without doubt, it denotes not merely freedom from bodily restraint but also *the right of the individual to contract, to engage in any of the common occupations of life, to acquire useful knowledge,* to marry, establish a home and bring up children, to worship God according to the dictates of his own conscience, and generally to enjoy those privileges long recognized at common law as essential to the orderly pursuit of happiness by free men."[17] The Court held that the Nebraska law was not a reasonable restriction on that "right to engage in any of the common occupations of life" and struck the law down. Unfortunately, the Supreme Court later rejected the whole doctrine of substantive due process in the 1937 case of *West Coast Hotel v. Parrish,* which left Carl Beazer without a strong doctrinal basis for challenging his firing for getting help with his drug problem.[18] But the idea that the Fourteenth Amendment was intended to protect social rights such as the opportunity to earn a living remains dormant in the U.S. constitutional tradition, ready to be resurrected as a privilege of U.S. citizenship. In fact, to do so would bring contemporary doctrine much closer to the original intent of the Fourteenth Amendment.

In fact, the Court should overturn the *Slaughterhouse Cases;* the right to earn a living should be a privilege of U.S. citizenship. It can be regulated for the public good, but it cannot arbitrarily be deprived by the state. One immediate effect of this action would be to enable Carl Beazer to challenge the New York City Transit Authority's regulation that caused him to be fired for trying to kick his drug habit. When the state deprives workers of their means of earning a living, it must provide a reasonable justification. If methadone users are bad employment risks, their termination is justified, but that was not true in Beazer's case. Courts should always show deference to the expertise of democratically elected officials, but a judge must make the final decision on a right of constitutional magnitude. Some will say this involves the federal judiciary unduly in the affairs of New York City. But the interference is no more than New York City already must accept when other fundamental rights, like free speech, are involved.[19] In any case, this was what the drafters of the Fourteenth Amendment intended; they believed certain rights, like the right to earn a living, were so important as to require federal judicial protection.

But protecting the Carl Beazers of the world is only a beginning; American society also must provide the millions of Americans without jobs the opportunity to earn a living. The "official" unemployment rate has oscillated between 4 percent and 8 percent since World War II. This means that tens of millions of Americans are regularly deprived of an opportunity to earn a living. This figure does not include those who are unable to find jobs—those who have stopped looking after continual failure and those who are able to find only part-time jobs. It does not include the millions of workers who are able to find only "temporary" work, which fails to provide the benefits that turn a job into a livelihood. It also does not include all the children whose parents are unable to find work and whose lives are scarred by this experience. A vibrant economy decreases the number but never solves the problem of unemployment. And holding a job does not necessarily translate into earning a living. The 1990s saw great economic growth, which helped most Americans financially, but as late as 1998 (the last year for which statistics are available) almost 40 percent of American families earned less than $25,000 per year.[20]

Society should never underestimate the importance of economic policies that support economic growth; a vibrant economy creates a tight labor market, which promotes the opportunity to earn a living more effectively than any government program. But policies that merely promote economic growth will always be inadequate if the goal is to provide jobs for all Americans willing to work. The market alone does not create enough jobs. Therefore overturning *Beazer* will not be enough to guarantee that all Americans enjoy the privilege of an opportunity to earn a living.

Does the unemployment of millions of Americans raise an issue of constitutional significance? This is a crucial decision for the future of constitutional theory, and the conventional answer is no. This response reflects two assumptions underlying most contemporary constitutional scholarship. The first is that constitutional law is strictly limited to "judicial review"—the determination of whether laws are constitutional or not. Constitutional law is never concerned with giving guidance as to what laws best fulfill the Constitution's goals. The second assumption is that the Constitution is primarily a charter of negative liberties that may sometimes protect citizens from government action but never requires the government to act affirmatively.

If readers accept these propositions, my thesis is dead on arrival because courts alone just do not have the power to reform democracy as I suggest. There must be legislative action if all Americans are to be offered an opportunity to pursue their vision of happiness, and that action must be affirmative in nature. The reigning constitutional consensus is really a unarticulated justification for the status quo.

Luckily, neither of the conventional assumptions has much historical or intellectual force behind it. Clearly, James Madison and the other signers would be shocked to hear that the role of the courts was the primary focus of constitutional law. Happenstance did not lead them to discuss judicial power in Article III after first setting out the roles of Congress in Article I and of the president in Article II. The framers saw the judiciary as the least dangerous branch of government because they expected it to be the least powerful of the three. The myopic focus of most constitutional theory on the role of courts reflects the guild needs of the lawyers who plead before the courts more than the original design of the Constitution. Courts have an important role to play in constitutional law, but it is clear that the founders intended the Constitution to be implemented by all three branches of government.[21]

A little reflection will show that the second assumption—that the Constitution is primarily a charter of negative liberties—is really merely a postulate of the first. It simply is not true that the Constitution does not call on government to take positive action; it clearly does. In fact, the objective of the whole constitutional enterprise was affirmative in nature. The preamble states the goals of the document explicitly: "[T]o form a more perfect Union, establish justice, insure domestic tranquility, provide for the common defense, promote the general welfare, and secure the blessings of liberty to ourselves and our posterity." I put special emphasis on the preamble's goal of "pro-

moting the general welfare." The verb *to promote* has no negative con-
notations, and the noun *welfare* or the adjective *general* cannot be
narrowly defined. And the goals are not limited to the preamble.
Article I, section 8, grants Congress the power to accomplish the goal
of promoting the general welfare: "The Congress shall have the power to lay and collect taxes . . . to pay the debts and provide for the
common defense and general welfare of the United States." Similarly, the authors of the Fourteenth Amendment clearly intended to
describe positive action to protect citizens.[22] This is evident in the
fifth section's affirmative grant of power to Congress to enforce the
Amendment's provisions. As I have shown, one of those provisions
was the promise in section 1 to protect the privileges or immunities
of American citizens. And one of those privileges was the opportunity to earn a living.

Now it is true that the privilege the authors of the Fourteenth
Amendment had in mind was a negative one. It protected the right
of an individual to pursue an occupation, not the duty of government to provide jobs for those willing to work. But a constitution
written in the eighteenth and nineteenth centuries must be interpreted dynamically if it is to serve citizens in the twenty-first century. The landmark case of *Goldberg v. Kelly* (1970) is a good example.
The Court had to decide whether rights to government programs like
welfare and social security were property under the due process
clause. The Court was aware that the term *property* was originally limited to interests in real property and other interests protected by common law, not government payments. But the Court realized that the
Constitution protected property in order to give the citizen a firm
base of economic independence. While that independence had come

from owning real estate in the eighteenth century, the right to receive government benefits like social security and welfare played that same structural role for many citizens in the twentieth century. Accordingly, the Court ruled that such entitlements to governments payments are property protected by the due process clause.[23]

The right to earn a living is a parallel situation. A negative right was adequate in the nineteenth century when the United States was primarily rural and had a shortage of workers, but today's economy does not spontaneously produce jobs for all those willing to work. In fact, high unemployment is a clearly foreseeable result of government economic policies. The unemployed are really victims of the war against inflation. The government raises interest rates in order to control inflation, but an indirect effect is a rise in unemployment. In this context, not to interpret the right to earn a living as a positive right would rob it of meaning for millions of Americans.

Of course, a court cannot issue an injunction requiring full employment; this is a task beyond judicial capacity. But it would be a grave mistake to limit constitutional rights to those that can be enforced judicially. That a fundamental right can be secured only by political mechanisms makes it no less fundamental in a constitutional sense. Constitutional theory's preoccupation with judicial review has concealed Congress's use of its authority under the spending power to provide Americans with the opportunity to earn a living. For instance, after the Civil War the Homestead Act awarded 160 acres to any citizen willing to work the land for five years. This was an attempt to implement the republican ideal of a free, independent citizen who earned his own livelihood. Earlier generations of the Joad family may have benefited from this affirmative government action.

When unemployment skyrocketed in the 1930s, Franklin Roosevelt and the New Deal Congress acted to provide citizens with the opportunity to earn a living. Congress established the Public Works Administration (PWA) in 1933 with an appropriation of \$3.3 billion, an enormous amount of money at the time. The goal was a double one, to improve America's infrastructure and provide decent jobs. It was successful on both counts. Not only did it provide five billion hours of employment but the PWA also added roads and highways, sewerage, water systems, gas and electric power plants, schools and courthouses, hospitals and jails, dams and canals, bridges and viaducts, and docks and tunnels to the nation's assets.[24]

New Deal programs like the PWA probably rescued some of the Joads; millions of Americans were the beneficiaries of yet another national work program: World War II. Never forget that the government's demand for labor and goods during the war ended the depression, not some internal "balance wheel" within the engine of capitalism. Remember too that no one spoke of "unqualified" workers; everyone was needed for the war effort.

In 1944, as World War II came to an end, Roosevelt called for a "Second Bill of Rights" that included "social rights." One was a "decent job."[25] At the time it did not seem like a radical proposal; it was an attempt to make good on a part of the American Dream as old as the Declaration of Independence's promise that all citizens be allowed to pursue their idea of happiness. And the GI Bill after the war was at least a partial fulfillment of that promise, because it permitted veterans to obtain a college education, which led to middle-class employment opportunities.

The opportunity to earn a living rests comfortably within Congress's power to spend for the general welfare as set out in Article I of the Constitution. The argument should not be about the goal but rather the most effective means of achieving it. But this is the line that divides constitutional theory and economic policy. This book may be able to provide a blueprint for American government, but it can never claim to be a manual in macroeconomic policy making. Still, some economic goals should not be controversial: keeping the unemployment rate as low as possible while controlling inflation; investing heavily in improving the skills of workers; and investing in the economic and social infrastructure of U.S. society, a investment that will pay off by providing not only a more competitive economy and more livable society but also by creating jobs.

But, unfortunately, even a robust economy will not provide all citizens with an opportunity to earn a living. Some are too old to work; others are disabled. These people receive support from social security and disability programs. And a dynamic economy will always require transitional unemployment as the market moves workers from one job category to another; unemployment insurance furnishes support for these workers. But one group of able-bodied adults and their children cannot support themselves at a minimum level of comfort without government assistance.

This group is sometimes referred to as the welfare population. I can state my stance on welfare succinctly: Everyone who is able to work should—but no one who works should be poor. If Thoreau wants to spend his days out at Walden Pond, that's fine so long as he does so at his own expense. But people who do choose to work should be able to achieve a modicum of material comfort. Making good on this simple philosophy would end welfare as we know it.

Clearly, attaining this goal requires more than one strategy; I will focus on one program proposed by two experts in the field, Mary Jo Bane and David Ellwood, because it illustrates that public policy experts believe that the goal of jobs for all Americans is not beyond this country's administrative or economic reach.[26]

Bane and Ellwood first suggest that the minimum wage be raised to a level at which a full-time minimum wage employee could support a family of four above the poverty level. This was the de facto U.S. policy up through the 1970s, but the minimum wage has failed to keep up with inflation since then. Of course, society must accept a trade-off between the benefits of a higher minimum wage and the loss of jobs that the increase indirectly causes. To the extent a further raise in the minimum wage is not practicable, Bane and Ellwood suggest expanding the Earned Income Tax Credit (EITC), a little-known reform that Congress enacted in 1990 and expanded in 1994. It could be expanded even further. For instance, for every dollar earned up to $10,000, a worker with two children could be given a 50 percent tax credit toward her or his federal tax liability. This credit would be refunded in cash if it exceeded actual tax liability. The credit then would be reduced incrementally for each dollar earned over $10,000, up to a final cutoff point, perhaps 150 percent of the poverty level. One advantage of the tax credit strategy is that it costs the employer nothing and therefore causes no loss of jobs. It could be combined with a raise in the minimum wage to achieve the goal of assuring that every full-time worker could support a family of four at a modest level of comfort.

"Welfare reform" in the 1990s was centered around helping recipients find jobs in the private economy. This is a worthwhile strategy if it is not administered in a punitive fashion. But it will never be enough to provide a job for all Americans willing to work. For those who fail to find jobs in the private economy, the government should provide jobs in the public sector. A minimum wage job should be offered to all willing to work. Once again, the historical parallel is the PWA experience of the 1930s. Now as then, myriad projects would improve the quality of life for all Americans as well as provide jobs for those who need them.

Is there any possibility that Congress today would adopt such a program? Probably not. But perhaps I can change some minds. Once Americans as a political community take full employment as a constitutional responsibility rather than merely a policy option, the dynamic for reform should gain momentum. The question becomes "how," not "if." And I would be wrong to minimize the rhetorical effect of the phrase "a right to earn a living." For instance, much of the U.S. political system's respect for freedom of speech is completely independent of any enforcement by the courts; once citizens became convinced that they possessed a right to free speech, the legislatures started to implement that right without prodding by the judiciary.[27]

Also, it is important to point out a synergy between the reforms that I recommend. Every citizen should have a decent job. Clearly, this goal is much easier to reach if each citizen is also given a good education, a reform I discuss in the next chapter. Americans may also find that the current Congress's insensitivity to the inability of millions of Americans to earn a decent living may only reflect the refusal of the system to respect other fundamental rights, such as free speech and the vote. For instance, full employment might become a more attainable political objective if affluent Americans did not have a monopoly on the financing of political campaigns, a topic I discuss in chapter 4. Similarly, retooling the U.S. electoral system to give every American a vote that counts should give low-income Americans greater political clout, which can transform apparently utopian ideals into realistic political options. This is the subject of chapter 5. And the synergy works the other way too. Reform of the political system will make full employment a mainstream goal, and people with jobs and a good education are more likely to become active participants in politics.

Of course, providing jobs for all Americans willing to work is not inexpensive. Programs such as the Earned Income Tax Credit deprive the treasury of tax receipts, but the other reforms necessary to enable parents with children to work will also require government-financed child care and medical care. As I detail in chapter 3, providing every American with a first-rate education also will be expensive. What I am proposing is costly. But so is tolerating the status quo. All sorts of social evils, from armed robbery to domestic abuse, are related to poverty. And the United States spends billions of dollars each year to incarcerate millions of Americans. This does not include the harm done the victims of crime or harm caused to families of criminals. So while reform is expensive it might be less expensive than maintaining the status quo. And the money is there. The federal tax surplus for the first decade of the twenty-first century is estimated at almost $2 trillion, and that's after another $2 trillion is set aside to bolster the social security system.[28]

But the statistics are of secondary importance. The key thing to remember is that the involuntarily unemployed are making a claim of right, not a plea for charity. The Constitution gives every American a right to certain basic privileges as members of the national political community. One of these privileges is the opportunity to earn a living. Not to honor that right is to dishonor the best in the American political tradition since 1776.

3

A First-Rate Education

In the bookshop, 1950s. Courtesy of Tony Stone Images/Chicago Inc.

In these days, it is doubtful that any child may reasonably be expected to succeed in life if he is denied the opportunity of an education.

—Chief Justice Earl Warren in *Brown v. Board of Education* (1954)

In chapter 1, I discussed the failure of parents in the Edgewood school district in San Antonio to convince the Supreme Court that the equal protection clause required that Texas institute a school-financing system that would provide their children with a first-rate education. The Court rested its decision on the proposition that education is not a fundamental right and therefore courts should show great deference to the decisions of the legislature in this area.

Reclaiming the privileges or immunities clause permits the reconsideration of whether the Supreme Court was correct in that decision as a matter of constitutional law. Education was not one of the specific rights that the authors of the Fourteenth Amendment had in mind when they sent the amendment to the states for ratification. The United States was still a primarily agricultural society, and hard work, rather than formal education, was seen as the prerequisite to financial independence. But the phrase "privileges or immunities" was never meant to be confined to a list of specific concrete mini-rights but instead referred to all the fundamental rights that made a person a citizen instead of a slave or a serf. It was meant to be a dynamic concept rather than a laundry list. Whatever the situation in the middle of the nineteenth century, clearly a first-rate education is an essential component of citizenship in the twenty-first century.

I pointed out in chapter 2 that after the Supreme Court's mutilation of the privileges or immunities clause in the 1873 *Slaughterhouse Cases,* the Court transplanted the ideology of fundamental rights from the privileges or immunities clause into the concept of liberty protected by the due process clause of the Fourteenth Amendment. Let me repeat the definition of *liberty* that the Court invoked in *Meyer v. Nebraska* (1923): "Without doubt, it denotes not merely freedom from bodily restraint but also the right of the individual to contract, to engage in any of the common occupations of life, *to acquire useful knowledge, to marry, to establish a home* and bring up children, to worship God according to the dictates of his own conscience, and generally to enjoy those privileges long recognized at common law as *essential to the orderly pursuit of happiness by free men.*"[1]

Of course, I must acknowledge that in *Meyer* (and, two years later, in *Pierce v. Society of Sisters*) the Court was speaking of a "negative" liberty.[2] As I explained in chapter 2, in regard to the right to earn a living, the circumstances faced by citizens in the twentieth and twenty-first centuries mean that Americans today must transform the negative liberty to a positive right and must make a similar change in regard to education. In fact, the claim to positive status of a right to a first-rate education is much stronger than the claim of a right to earn a living. The affirmative right to government-financed employment is still a controversial issue in the United States, but the right to a state-financed education is not. In fact, the Supreme Court conceded that point in *San Antonio v. Rodriguez,* where it suggested that the state's complete refusal to offer a public school education would violate the equal protection clause.[3] It is simply unthinkable that a modern democracy would play no affirmative role in educating its citizens.

There are two points to emphasize in regard to the definition of *liberty* that the Court used in *Meyer.* First, note how the Court connects *liberty* with *privileges,* which it then sees as essential to "the orderly pursuit of happiness by free men." Here the Court is injecting in the due process clause basic substantive rights that it sees as necessary to fulfilling the Declaration of Independence's description of the "unalienable right" to the "pursuit of happiness." Second, *Meyer* expanded the list of fundamental rights to include both the right to "acquire useful knowledge" and the right to "establish a home and bring up children." Both rights imply a right to a good education: formal schooling is the usual way of "acquiring knowledge," and providing a good education is one of the primary means of "bringing up children." This connection between education and a citizen's right to raise children was made even more explicit in the Supreme Court's decision in *Pierce.* There the Supreme Court held that an Oregon statute, which effectively closed private schools, violated the "liberty of parents and guardians to direct the upbringing and education of the children under their control."[4]

In a 1937 case the Supreme Court rejected the doctrine of substantive due process upon which both the *Meyer* and *Pierce* opinions relied.[5] But once again, the constitutional force of the ideology of fundamental rights was not dammed, only diverted to the channels of another constitutional text. In 1954 the Court used the equal protection clause to protect fundamental rights. This is how Chief Justice Earl Warren discusses the role of education in American society in his landmark opinion in the case of *Brown v. Board of Education:* "It is the very foundation of good citizenship. Today it is a principal instrument in awakening the child to cultural values, in preparing him for later professional training, and in helping to adjust normally to his environment. In these days, it is doubtful that any child may reasonably be expected to succeed in life if he is denied the opportunity of an education."[6]

One would think that the constitutional guarantee of a first-rate education to every American would not be a controversial issue. Who, after all, is against education? And it does not, in contrast to the promise of a job to those willing to work, have even faintly socialist overtones; rather, it is in complete harmony with the American credo of equal opportunity for all. Yet, as I pointed out in chapter 1, the Supreme Court refused to find education to be a fundamental right in *San Antonio v. Rodriguez.*

The tension between the Supreme Court's treatment of education in the cases of *Brown* and *San Antonio v. Rodriguez* is stark. I have no qualms about resolving that tension in favor of *Brown.* But this still leaves the question of what the core "meaning" of *Brown* is. The case involved the intentional segregation of the races in the public schools of Topeka, Kansas. The Court held the segregation unconstitutional, but why it did so is open to interpretation. *Brown* can be read as a discrimination case, the one that rejected state-enforced racial segregation as unconstitutional, not only in schools but in all public services. The government should never label its citizens by race. This is certainly one proper reading of *Brown,* and the case must be judged a success on this dimension. As I discuss in chapter 6, the United States still has enormous problems involving race, but the principle against invidious racial labeling is firmly established.

Brown can also be considered a school integration case, the one that held that every American child deserves to be educated in a racially integrated environment. This reading of *Brown* has never been realized. In part it has been the victim of later decisions of the Supreme Court.[7] But this interpretation also is somewhat in conflict with the principle articulated in cases like *Pierce*—that it is the right of the parent, not the state, to direct the child's education. Parents have a constitutional right to send their children to private schools. And since the 1960s they have increasingly exercised that right to the extent that, between the exodus to racially homogeneous public school districts and the growth in popularity of private schools, there simply are not enough white children left in many large urban school districts to permit a racially integrated education.

That situation is unfortunate because all children benefit from going to school with children from a wide variety of racial, ethnic, and social backgrounds. The parents spending enormous amounts of money to raise their children in a hothouse atmosphere where they do not interact with youngsters from different racial and class backgrounds are doing them a disservice, but it is their constitutional right to make that choice. Those who disagree must convince them of the superiority of an integrated education. A third reading of *Brown* may be helpful in doing so. Some middle-class white parents choosing private schools or moving to the suburbs are not fleeing racial minorities but inferior public schools. Guaranteeing every American child a first-rate public education would also promote an integrated education.

I would interpret *Brown* as promising each American child a first-rate education as a privilege of national citizenship. In doing so I rely on Warren's statement in *Brown* that "it is doubtful that any child may reasonably be expected to succeed in life if he is denied the opportunity of an education."[8] This is a recognition that a good education is one of those fundamental rights guaranteed to all citizens. So interpreted, *Brown* holds that the minority children in Topeka, Kansas, were deprived of two separate rights. First, they were deprived of equal protection of the laws because the school district's policy of intentional racial segregation labeled them as inferior on account of their race. But they were also deprived of a privilege of American citizenship—the right to a first-rate education—because of the inferior schools they were forced to attend. Of course, the *Brown* opinion does not use the adjective *first-rate;* it refers only to the opportunity for an education. But I infer that the Court meant "first-rate" from its comment that "it is doubtful that than any child may reasonably be expected to succeed in life if he is denied the opportunity of an education."[9] This goal of success in life, so consistent with the promise of the Declaration of Independence, cannot be achieved by just any education; certainly, it cannot be achieved by exposure to the educational opportunities Jonathan Kozol witnessed at East St. Louis High. A realistic chance for success requires a first-rate education. I define "a first-rate education" as one that permits the student to compete successfully in the economic marketplace and to effectively participate in the governance of our democracy. I see it much more like the education that suburban children received in Alamo Heights than that provided their inner-city peers in the Edgewood district of San Antonio. It is not a right that depends on race; it looks instead to the quality of the education the state provides.

Critics are likely to lodge two objections to a federal constitutional right to a first-rate education. The first would warn against the intrusion of the federal government in the domain of education, traditionally a local responsibility. The short reply to this objection is that the states approved the Fourteenth Amendment because they agreed that certain rights were too important to leave to local discretion. It also is pure myth to think that education is any longer merely a matter of local concern. Not only is a well-educated workforce a matter of national concern but local school districts have been receiving significant federal financial support for a long time. Further, the privileges or immunities clause of the Fourteenth Amendment does not substitute the federal government for local school districts; it merely insists that the federal government monitor the states to ensure that they provide all citizens with the privileges the amendment protects—including a first-rate education.

The second objection goes to the capacity of courts to monitor state education bureaucracies. The problem with arguing that courts have no role to play in ensuring that children receive a first-rate education is that state courts, such as those in New Jersey and Connecticut, have required reform of their school-financing systems in order to fulfill the mandates of their state constitutions.[10] But courts alone will never be able to provide an excellent education for all children. As I showed in chapter 2 in regard to the right to earn a living, courts will have to act in concert with legislatures and administrators; courts' exact role will vary depending on the issue involved.

I might tentatively divide the issues surrounding educational reform into three categories: financial reform, structural reform, and access. The role of the judiciary will change with each issue. For example, a good education requires money. This does not mean that money itself guarantees success, anymore than money guarantees success in finding a cure for a disease or fighting a war; as the philosophers say, it may not be a sufficient condition for success, but it is a necessary one.

A given in discussing school financing should be that each American child has the same amount of dollars allotted to her or his education. Recall that in *San Antonio v. Rodriguez,* the rich, suburban, mostly white school district was permitted to spend almost twice as many dollars per child as the poor, urban, heavily minority district. This is an outrageous situation but, unfortunately, not an uncommon one.

Most state school-financing schemes are based on each school district's taxing the property within its borders. Because each state has property-rich and property-poor districts, the result is wide disparities between districts in taxable wealth. While it is not true that all poor children live in property-poor districts, for the most part the correlation between the wealth of a district and the wealth of its residents is strong. The plaintiffs in *San Antonio v. Rodriguez* asked the Supreme Court to rule the that the equal protection clause of the Fourteenth Amendment required Texas to cut the connection between school financing and the proceeds of local property tax. The Supreme Court refused to do so, and that decision should now be overturned. The Fourteenth Amendment does not talk about school districts; it talks about the duties of states.

The goal of equal expenditures for each child is a good slogan but really should be seen more as a starting point than an ultimate goal. Equal expenditures may not be enough to provide an equal education. For instance, an urban school with an antiquated physical plant might see its money used disproportionately for maintenance, or a school with a high enrollment of students in need of special education might need additional funding if it is to provide an education of equal quality to all its students. In addition, children from poor homes where academic skills are not emphasized will need special attention if they are to receive a first-rate education. Such differences between schools and their student bodies require differential funding. This will always create vexing administrative problems in deciding how much to compensate a district for the special expenses it must incur, but these problems are manageable within a system that holds to the basic principle of equal funding for each child, tempered by reasonable adjustments for special needs.

So the first step in implementing the national privilege of a first-rate education would be to require that states provide equal funding for each child's education unless an inequality in expenditure can be justified on educational grounds. Courts could effectively monitor this requirement, which would, in effect, overturn *San Antonio v. Rodriguez*. This would be an important beginning but just a beginning. Another problem is the shocking disparities in funding between states. Just as rich suburban school districts spend as much as twice what poor urban districts in the same state spend, so rich northeastern states spend as much as three times what poor southern states spend to educate a child. For instance, New Jersey spent $9,700 per child in 1996 (the last year for which statistics are available), while Mississippi spent only $3,700 per child.[11] This means that while both New Jersey and Mississippi students are ostensibly being prepared to compete for positions in the same national and international labor market, the New Jersey students receive a giant (and unjustifiable) head start. The situation becomes even more striking when comparing both interstate and intrastate differences in spending. Consider the gulf in spending, for instance, between the most affluent New Jersey suburb and the poorest Mississippi rural school district.[12] Yet the children in both districts share U.S. citizenship.

If the right to a good education is a privilege of U.S. citizenship, this disparity makes no sense at all. Mississippi children deserve the same quality of education as New Jersey children. Once again, we need not be blind to regional differences in the cost of living or other factors that might justify disparities between states, but the principle remains clear—equal spending on the education of every American child, unless some inequality in expenditure can be justified to the satisfaction of the federal judiciary.

Still, all this talk of equality begs the most important question of all: What does it cost to provide a first-rate education? It would be shortsighted merely to average out the current expenditures of the various states. Many of these states have a long history of miserly spending on education. It would make more sense to take a state with high expenditures like New Jersey and see what services it provides its children. These services should be available to all American children.

No matter what the method used, this is a question beyond the institutional capacity of the courts; it is Congress's responsibility to determine what financial resources are necessary to provide each American child with a first-rate education and to make sure that such resources are available. Some of the fiscal responsibility would remain with the individual states, but Congress could use its authority under the spending power of Article I and under section 5 of the Fourteenth Amendment to place its fiscal muscle behind the states' efforts. This type of state-federal cooperation was a staple of American federalism during most of the twentieth century, and it is completely in harmony with the text and structure of the Fourteenth Amendment.

But, of course, money is never by itself enough. It is necessary to go beyond the question of adequate funding to consider what institutional structures best promote a good education. Jonathan Kozol's experience at East St. Louis High illustrates that point. Lack of money was a big problem; a school that cannot afford to put a crossbar on a goalpost cannot provide an excellent education. Other problems at East St. Louis High included a cavernous building inhabited by dispirited students and a depressed faculty. But East St. Louis High need not be the future of American public education. Innovative models exist.

Let me make a short digression to contrast what Jonathan Kozol found on his visit to East St. Louis High with my own experience while visiting Vanguard High School in New York City, a school in many ways similar to East St. Louis High—and in many wonderful ways quite different. I realize that it is unusual for a book on constitutional law to discuss teaching methods at a public high school, but I think it is an important addition to the discussion of adequate school funding. Taxpayers reasonably are reluctant to generously fund schools that fail to educate well; Vanguard High School demonstrates that inner-city publics schools can succeed.

East St. Louis High and Vanguard High are both urban high schools with a student population of poor and mostly minority students. Vanguard, however, is part of an educational reform movement within the New York City School District. This district was created to administer Vanguard and several other experimental junior high and high schools, all of which are housed in buildings that formerly were home to mammoth school populations but now have been divided up and house two or more smaller schools in the same building.

The educational philosophy behind these new schools holds that "small" schools are pedagogically superior to "large" schools. Small schools allow teachers to engage each other on issues of pedagogy, whereas large schools rely on bureaucratic rules that teachers find constricting and alienating. The smaller schools also permit more room for experiments and for quickly modifying experiments that do not work. Small schools, with their less formal administrative structures, also work better for parents, allowing them to get to know their children's teachers in a way that a rushed parents' night in a three-thousand-pupil school can never hope to match.

Most important is that schools like Vanguard work for the students. I think the main reason is that the teachers get to know the students as individuals and therefore can tailor the school experience to meet the individual student's needs. Well-meaning middle-class people tend to picture students from poor backgrounds as just like middle-class children. Children from poor backgrounds, although they come to school with native ability equal to that of their middle-class peers, often have little awareness of that ability or of the opportunities hard work in school can create for them. Someone has to convince them that the educational game is worth the effort, that school can be an avenue for the pursuit of happiness. Each student needs to develop a consciousness of possibility—imagining a better state of affairs than the present and a belief in the possibility of attaining it.[13] Only a teacher who possesses this consciousness can impart it to students.

My first stop at Vanguard was Marian Mogulescu's class. My visit was in the middle of June, and she was monitoring about fifteen students who were completing their work for the school year. One student (let's call him Tito) was particularly distracted and distracting. You didn't need to be an educational psychologist to see that Tito was edgy; he appeared to like the teachers and the other students (and Mogulescu later told me he was very bright), but he was extremely restless. Of course, during the last couple weeks of the school year, suburban schools also have many restless male teenagers, but something more than hormones and spring fever appeared to be affecting Tito. School was "OK" but at some level he felt the gravitational pull of "the street," where part of him expected to end up. His teacher's job was help Tito see that he could graduate and go on to college. She worked at it by alternately cajoling Tito and seducing him with humor and praise. The clear message to Tito (and me) was that she knew him and liked him but was not going to put up with his nonsense. I think the key was that he knew that she cared for him and believed he could succeed if he worked.

I witnessed another dividend of personal involvement that morning. When I arrived, the police had just picked up two students.

Within minutes other students had notified faculty, and the head teacher was on the phone to intercede with the police. The problem turned out to be a misunderstanding, which was quickly cleared up once the officers could talk to a responsible adult who could vouch for the students. A phone call from an assistant principal who had no personal knowledge of the students would never have gotten the job done. It seems to me that this personal knowledge provides students much more security than any metal detector can provide.

At Vanguard the emphasis is on critical thinking. Each year the school focuses on one of three themes: growth, law, or the environment. Before graduation each student does work in all three areas. And each area includes many traditional disciplines. For instance, when law is the theme, students explore the laws of motion (physics) as well as the U.S. Constitution. They also engage in projects that test their ability to apply book learning to new contexts. For instance, a student might design a water ride at an amusement park to demonstrate mastery of physics or participate in a mock trial involving the expulsion of a student for possession of drugs to demonstrate mastery of constitutional law. All projects are graded on a four-point scale. Although the school prefers individual evaluation to traditional pencil-and-paper tests, Mogulescu says the standards are no less rigorous than those used at traditional schools. Before graduation each student must make a senior presentation of projects in each of nine curricular areas.

As a student finishes a project, it goes into his or her "portfolio," which the faculty reviews periodically. Each student's portfolio slowly expands over the years as graduation approaches. This method allows teachers to monitor a student's performance. The portfolio is also tangible evidence of progress, which gives the student a feeling of accomplishment deeper than that provided by only test grades. It also provides students with something to show prospective employers and college admissions officers. The day I visited, a recent graduate who had just finished her first year at Syracuse University came back to show the younger students her portfolio. They seemed very impressed by it and even more that she was succeeding at college.

Educational "structure" has other important aspects. One is what courses should be taught. Debates about educational policy usually invoke "The Canon." Many conservatives argue that every American child must be familiar with certain works. For better or for worse, Americans have never been able to agree on which works qualify for this list. The historian Lawrence Levine has demonstrated exactly how porous the concept of an "American canon" has been for the last two hundred years. He notes that two editions of the same book published years apart listed eight or nine consensus choices as "American classics," but only three works made both lists.[14]

The content of the American canon will always be contested territory, and perhaps it should be in a democracy. An effective curriculum can be traditional or experimental so long as it makes sense from the student's perspective. Of course, the canon should include excellent works by authors once ignored because they are minorities, but that does not mean that Shakespeare is irrelevant to the problems students face today. At Vanguard *Macbeth* peacefully coexists with Toni Morrison's *The Bluest Eye*. The pedagogical goal in reading either work is the same—teaching the student how to think.

The Syracuse sophomore's visit to her old high school highlights another important point about providing a good education: it has to lead somewhere. One reason low-income high school students have a problem taking high school seriously is that they cannot link it to any realistic future for themselves. If a high school degree is insufficient to land a good job, and college is not realistic possibility, what is the incentive to work hard in school? Thus the Vanguard alumna's visit played a double function. First, students saw the staff treat her as a VIP of whom the school was very proud. And the younger students could see that being a student was not a dead-end occupation—it could lead to an exciting new life.

Vanguard High School adopts a "college prep" approach to education, and it seems to work. But for many students from poor backgrounds, college may appear to be an unattainable goal; they may require an approach that helps them to use high school as a stepping-stone to a good-paying job or higher education. The Biotech Academy at Berkeley High and at Fremont High in Oakland, California, attempts to provide just such a "school-to-career" program. The programs are run by the nonprofit Berkeley Biotechnology Education, Inc. (BBEI), in conjunction with Berkeley High School and Fremont High, and feeds graduates to Laney Junior College. BBEI chooses participants in the summer before their junior year in high school. The students chosen tend to be "academically fragile," youngsters with a higher-than-average risk of dropping out of high school. The students are lured into the program by the promise of summer employment in the biotech industry between their junior and senior years. The students take a special science-loaded curriculum in their last two years of high school, which coordinates their academic labors with the hands-on experience provided by their summer internships.

Upon graduation some students have amassed sufficient high school credits to permit them to enter a four-year college if they choose that route. Others leave school at this point and take jobs in the booming East Bay biotech industry; this in itself is a vast improvement on the employment prospects for graduates; recall that some graduates of East St. Louis High were being prepared for jobs at McDonald's. Most of the BBEI grads, however, choose to continue their studies in the biotech program at Laney College's Biotech Career Institute. While at Laney they are provided with part-time jobs in the biotech industry that not only supplement their academic studies but also provide much-needed income. Upon completion of the one-year curriculum at Laney, the students can use the program's job placement program to find a job in the biotech industry. The program's graduates have proved highly employable, finding jobs with beginning annual salaries as high as $35,000. About half the students continue their studies while employed.

Vanguard High School and the Berkeley Biotech Academy at Berkeley and Fremont High Schools are only two examples of new, innovative approaches to education now being tried in public schools. How to provide a good education for every American child is no mystery. The list of educational reforms that have been shown to work is well known: strong preschool programs for youngsters at risk, more individual attention for students in the early years in reading and math, smaller classes, smaller schools, more special programs for students who fall behind, better qualified teachers, and more professional training for teachers.

The reform least discussed by politicians is raising teacher salaries, most likely because it is the most expensive. Yet the single most important ingredient in providing a first-rate education to every American child is making sure that talented teachers enter and remain in the profession. High school teachers in their forties who hold a master's degree (exactly the people the teaching profession needs) earn about $43,000 a year, whereas people with master's degrees in other fields earn an average of almost $76,000; the $33,000 difference is a penalty for choosing a teaching career. And the situation is getting worse—master's degree holders in other fields increased their salaries by an average $17,000 between 1994 and 1998; the salaries of teachers who hold master's degrees rose only $200.[15] Although the public school system has many dedicated and talented teachers like Marian Mogulescu despite the low pay, they will never be enough. In this country you get what you pay for. If Americans want the most talented students to become teachers, they are going to have to pay teachers like the middle-class professionals they are.

The final issue is that of access to higher education. Education at the college level and beyond is now part of the American Dream. No one cannot expect the students at Vanguard High (or East St. Louis High) to take school seriously if it only leads to a job at McDonald's. While courts cannot play a major role in how schools are structured, including the size of classes and the content of courses, they do have an important role to play in monitoring admissions policies.

In chapter 6, I discuss the important 1978 case of *Regents of the University of California v. Bakke*.[16] I argue that *Bakke* also is an education case, raising the issue of what the state owes an applicant to its medical school. I conclude that any applicants denied admission have been presumptively denied their right to a first-rate education.

The privilege of a first-rate education does not stop at high school; it continues as far as the student is able to take it. This does not mean that every applicant to medical school has a right to admission. Just like the butchers in the *Slaughterhouse Cases* and the subway employee in the *Beazer* case, medical school applicants have a right to fair admission procedures. If California medical schools decide that an applicant does not meet the qualifications for admission, they must explain why and justify the fairness of those qualifications.

Courts must take special care to see that supposedly neutral admissions procedures at both the undergraduate and graduate levels do not turn away applicants on the basis of class and race. For example, courts should investigate whether the SAT is overused in college admissions. It is instructive to compare the efficacy of the SAT and class rank as standards of college admission. The SAT is no more reliable a standard for measuring success in the first year of college than high school grades. Yet the use of the SAT does hurt the chances of acceptance of minority and low-income students.[17] If we are looking at an indicator of success in later life, the SAT is less helpful than high school grades because the SAT does not test so much of what contributes to good grades (study habits, perseverance, and the like). Most important, if society wants to choose an admissions system that makes most sense to students, class rank wins hands down. Class rank incorporates work from four years and is very much influenced by effort. The SAT takes three hours and appears to students to have as much connection with effort as the lottery.

Choosing students by class rank compares students on the basis of how they competed with students of similar backgrounds; that is the closest thing to a level playing field that is available. It would give a strong incentive to the best students in the "poor" high schools (who now might not be accepted even if they were at the top of their class), and to middle-class parents to send their children to those high schools, creating a voluntary form of class and racial integration in public high schools. The University of Texas has adopted such an approach, granting admission to the top 10 percent of every Texas high school class. The results have been a dramatic change in the makeup of the entering class at UT.[18]

But changing admission procedures will not be enough. Students from weak high schools will need "bridge" programs to prepare them to compete with students from more advantaged backgrounds once they get to college. One large problem is that bright students from poor school districts simply are not prepared for college. Also, bright graduates from poor schools have never been forced to cultivate the study habits necessary to succeed in college. In both instances the graduates of these schools, even if they are as gifted as their college classmates from rich schools, are not being given an equal chance at success. The university has to take action to level the playing field.

Americans traditionally think of private colleges as the turf of the upper-middle class and the wealthy, whereas working-class students attend the "free" public universities. All this has changed since the 1970s. Now private colleges draw their student bodies almost entirely from the middle, upper-middle, and upper classes, but so do public colleges and universities.[19] And these colleges, while still a value compared to private schools, are anything but free. This closes out the poor in two ways. First, fewer spots in the entering class are available to them, and college is increasingly expensive. Once again the answer is not difficult in an intellectual sense. The solution is need-based scholarships and living allowances for the top students from every high school.

If this all sounds expensive, it is. But whatever the expense of ensuring that every child receives a good education, Americans should consider three facts before allowing expense to be an excuse for not acting. First, consider the role of education in the lives of citizens in the twenty-first century. Isn't it hypocritical to use terms like "pursuit of happiness" and "equality of opportunity," so essential to Americans' sense of the United States, without providing each child with a first-rate education? Second, consider the expense of providing such an education within the context of a $300 billion defense budget. Bombers cost $30 million per plane. I do not raise these facts to challenge the wisdom of these enormous expenditures on defense but to make the less controversial point that when Americans are convinced of the need for a program, expense alone is never an insurmountable obstacle. A final fact to consider is the cost of continuing the status quo. In chapter 2 I discussed the connection between poverty and crime. The same arguments apply to education. Poor schools also cost taxpayers plenty.

4 A Voice That's Heard

Speaker, 1941. Courtesy of Tony Stone Images/Chicago Inc.

Those who won our independence believed that the final end of the State was to make men free to develop their faculties; and that in its government the deliberative forces should prevail over the arbitrary . . . that the greatest menace to freedom is an inert people; that public discussion is a political duty; and that this should be a fundamental principle of the American government.

—Justice Louis Brandeis in *Whitney v. California*

Let me summarize my argument up to this point. An interpretation of the Fourteenth Amendment that is faithful to its authors' vision would yield a series of privileges of American citizenship that would include certain social rights such as the opportunity to earn a living and the right to a first-rate education. These are affirmative rights owed to every U.S. citizen. The price for making these rights a reality might be high, but because these are matters of constitutional right, not legislative discretion, they must be honored.

Even if one finds intellectual merit in these proposals, they must sound absurdly utopian in the context of contemporary U.S. politics. In fact, candor requires that I acknowledge no realistic chance exists that the current political system would adequately fund the proposals I offer in chapters 2 and 3.

But now the argument takes another tack. Instead of despairing about the wrongheadedness of the current political system, I say let's reform it. Rather than abandon the quest to implement these social rights, which ring so true to the promise of the Declaration of Independence, let us insist on the full implementation of the political rights—free speech and the vote—that will facilitate implementation of these social rights. The present system's hostility to enlarging the social rights of Americans, like providing decent jobs and good schools, may reflect only its failure to honor a generous conception of these two political privileges of U.S. citizenship.

The synergy between political and social rights works in both directions: having full political rights increases the likelihood of gaining legislation that implements social rights; and a realistic possibility of enacting social legislation provides the incentive for the broad political participation necessary for legislative success. This chapter considers free speech. In chapter 5, I will discuss the right to vote.

The privileges or immunities clause was intended to incorporate the major guarantees of the Bill of Rights, including freedom of speech.[1] Of course, this does not advance the argument very far because current Supreme Court doctrine holds that the First Amendment's guarantee of free speech is also incorporated in the due process clause of Fourteenth Amendment.[2] So U.S. citizens have free speech rights; the difficult issue is determining what the oracular term *freedom of speech* means.

I will not pretend to give a comprehensive theory of free speech; my interest is in a smaller subset of speech practices, those that have a direct effect on the political process. In other words, I am primarily interested in political speech because this type of speech is directly relevant to implementing such privileges as the opportunity to earn a living and to receive a first-rate education.

But neither am I able to give full consideration to all the aspects of political speech in the short space allotted. Therefore, I will content myself with addressing two important issues. The first is the speech rights of citizens in what is called the public forum—streets, sidewalks, parks, and so on. This type of speech is important to individuals and groups that do not have access to large amounts of money, groups like the homeless coalition in the *Clark* case, discussed in chapter 1, that wanted to sleep in tents in the park across the street from the White House to protest government policy. A group that can afford full-page advertisements in the *New York Times* does not need to sleep in the park, but most citizens, or groups of citizens, cannot afford that form of speech.

The second issue involves government regulation of contributions to and expenditures by political campaigns. Here the problem is not that poor people are unable to speak but that rich people are able to speak too much. So while the fundamental constitutional issue is the same—how to ensure that all citizens possess a voice that is heard—I will show that a different remedy is necessary in each instance.

First, the issue of citizen speech in the public forum. The current Supreme Court's view of free speech is very much influenced by a famous metaphor for free speech introduced by Justice Oliver Wendell Holmes in his dissent in *Abrams v. U.S.* in 1919: "[T]*he test of truth is the power of the thought to get itself accepted in the competition of the market* and . . . truth is the only ground upon which [the people's] wishes safely can be carried out."[3] Holmes's idea was that American society must let the "marketplace" determine whether an idea has value; the government cannot be allowed to make that decision. The listener, not the government, should decide what is a good idea, just as the consumer, not the government, should decide what is a good product.

The metaphor of the marketplace of ideas is good as far as it goes; unfortunately, it does not go far enough. It argues for strong protection against intentional state censorship but has much less bite when the evil of purposeful suppression of speech is not present. The marketplace metaphor sees little need for judicial intervention if the government "unintentionally" interferes with the speech marketplace to achieve some policy goal unrelated to speech. For instance, if a group of students were suspended from a public high school for singing "We Shall Overcome" in the schoolyard to protest what they saw as racist school policies, their free speech rights would depend almost wholly on how the judge interpreted the principal's motives in ordering the suspension. If the students could show that the principal objected to the song's lyrics, the marketplace theory would grant the students strong protection. But if a judge decided the principal's motive was to make sure that the noise level of the singing did not disturb classes, the court could grant little protection because the intent was not censorship.

The result was what is sometimes called a two-track approach to free speech.[4] If the government is trying to block the message of speech, courts exercise very close scrutiny; if the state is interested in some goal other than suppressing speech, the courts tend to use a much gentler form of scrutiny. This approach contains two basic flaws. First is the problem of what might be called covert censorship; maybe the "disturbing classes" justification was only a pretext, and the reality was that the principal was angry that the students were accusing the school—and therefore the principal—of racism. The second flaw is even more serious. Even assuming that the principal had no ulterior motives, the students were still suspended for expressing their views on a public issue. In other words, the interference with free speech was the same no matter what the principal's motive was. Yet strong protection is limited to situations in which a bad motive is shown.

The Supreme Court's ruling in *Clark v. Community for Creative Non-violence,* one of the cases I discussed in chapter 1, is a good example of how the Supreme Court handles free speech issues today.[5] This was the 1984 case involving protesters who wanted to sleep in a national park and were denied permission to do so on the ground that sleeping constituted camping, which was prohibited under National Park Service rules. Once the Supreme Court was convinced that the park service was not banning the demonstration because it opposed the protesters' message, the justices readily deferred to the bureaucracy.

The Court's approach results in a very lopsided First Amendment, one that is highly protective of speech in theory but much less so in practice. The Court comes down heavily against laws aimed at the message of speech but reacts quite mildly to laws with other intentions. But in terms of numbers, the seemingly more benign group of laws is far larger than those aimed at the message of speech. Moreover, the distinction between those laws that are motivated by an intent to suppress and those that are not is a fine one, allowing judges to categorize laws as unintentional restrictionists of speech when they may in fact be covert attempts to silence unpopular speech. For instance, would the park service have been more hospitable to permitting sleeping in the park if the Girl Scouts had asked to camp out to honor the hundredth anniversary of the founding of the national park system? The Court's approach is consistent with the marketplace of ideas metaphor because laws not directed at suppressing the message of speech do not represent purposeful attempts by government to tamper with the free speech market. But they limit citizens' speech no less.

I argue for a more ambitious vision of free speech than the marketplace metaphor permits. Fortunately, Justice Louis Brandeis's famous concurrence in *Whitney v. California* (1927) provides inspiration for just such a vision:

> Those who won our independence believed that the final end of the State was to make men free to develop their faculties; *and in its government the deliberative forces should prevail over the arbitrary.* They believed in liberty both as an end and as a means. They believed liberty to be the secret of happiness and courage to be the secret of liberty. They believed that freedom to think as you will and to speak as you think are means indispensable to the discovery and spread of political truth; that without free speech and assembly discussion would be futile; that with them, discussion affords ordinarily adequate protection against the dissemination of noxious doctrine; *that the greatest menace to freedom is an inert people; that public discussion is a political duty; and that should be the fundamental principle of the American government.*[6]

Like Holmes, Brandeis condemns government censorship ("discussion affords ordinarily adequate protection against noxious doctrine") but makes no mention of the marketplace of ideas.[7] Brandeis's emphasis is on the necessity for a wide-ranging democratic colloquy in which the "deliberative forces should prevail over the arbitrary."[8] Although free speech is not exclusively limited to politics, the essential role of speech in the process of democratic deliberation provides the primary justification for its constitutional protection. Brandeis saw democracy as a system in which wide-ranging citizen discussions, not brute financial power, constitute the primary decision-making tool in a democracy. Citizens discuss public issues as civic equals, and then they vote as civil equals. This is how the historian Philippa Strum summarizes Brandeis's view of democracy: "He viewed democracy as free citizens making intelligent choices about matters affecting their joint lives. 'Free' citizens were those who were economically independent and who had a voice and vote in matters involving their political and economic well-being."[9] It is hard to imagine a better summary of the ideals I am championing here.

Brandeis, like Holmes, despised censorship, but Brandeis believed that government had to do more than merely restrain itself from tampering with the marketplace of ideas—he felt it had a duty to foster the public discussion essential to democracy because, as he put it, "the greatest menace to freedom is an inert people; . . . public discussion is a political duty; and . . . this should be a fundamental principle of the American government."[10]

Yet an inspiring vision is not enough; American society also needs a methodology for applying that idea to individual cases like *Clark*. Free speech methodology must recognize that the right of free speech can never be an absolute; it must be balanced against other important government goals. Of course, the term *balance* is itself a metaphor; no constitutional scale exists by which to objectively weigh speech against other values. It would be more accurate to say courts must mediate the demands of free speech and other government goals, attempting to harmonize the goal of maximizing citizen speech with other important policies. When government does take action that impedes citizen speech, a court must decide whether the state has adequately justified that loss of the speech opportunity. Even when the state is attempting to achieve an important state objective, a judge must ask whether the government has chosen the method of achieving it that has the least effect upon speech.

The First Amendment demands the most strenuous effort to reconcile the national commitment to speech with the desire to fulfill other government goals. Of course, some trade-off usually occurs between maximizing speech opportunities for citizens and effectively performing other government functions. Sometimes the choice is between more citizen speech and better park maintenance. But such a balancing act is inescapable in order to remain faithful to both the commitment to free speech and the need for efficient government.

This is where the Supreme Court went wrong in the *Clark* case. The speech involved the most political of speech—citizens asking their government for redress of grievances. It took place in a public park, a site that has always been a haven for free speech activity. More important, the park service did not have to choose between maintaining the grass and shrubbery and respecting the homeless coalition's free speech rights because both goals could be achieved. The park service could have protected the grass and shrubbery by simply enforcing "housekeeping" regulations such as forbidding the trampling of grass or littering. It did not have to ban sleeping to achieve this. In refusing to require the park service to adopt the alternative more friendly to free speech, the Court deprived the homeless coalition of a voice that is heard.

To summarize, my approach and that taken by the contemporary Supreme Court in cases like *Clark* differ in two important ways. I contend that a regulation passed with a "good motive" may interfere with free speech just as much as one passed with a "bad motive." Also, it is essential that the Court make sure that the legislature and the bureaucracy have done their best to maximize speech opportunities. This, of course, requires a balance between respect for speech and accomplishment of other important government functions, but only the Court is authorized to do the weighing. While it need not always rule in favor of the free speech claimant, it must make sure that the legislature has chosen the effective policy option most congenial to speech.

Clark is a situation in which a court must act in order to ensure that citizens have a vote that counts. Other times it is necessary that legislatures act in order to attain that same goal. The urgent need for campaign finance reform cries out for such action.

Monied interests provide most of the money that candidates for public office spend on their election campaigns. Campaign spending in 1996 was estimated to be as high as $1 billion, most of which came from wealthy contributors with financial interests in government action. One wealthy contributor was Roger Tamraz, an oilman who at least exhibited the virtue of candor. He acknowledged that he hoped his donations, totaling $300,000, to various arms of Bill Clinton's reelection campaign would buy him influence. Tamraz was able to gain access to the White House seven times. He readily agreed that this special access resulted from his contributions. Otherwise, as he told Senate investigators, he was wasting his money. Had he thought it a good investment? He said that next time he'd give $600,000. Asked whether he had voted in 1996, Tamraz replied that he had not bothered; he said he felt contributing money was the more effective route to being heard.[11]

Tamraz is undoubtedly correct. Which is more likely to get a politician's attention, one vote or a donation of $300,000 that the candidate can spend on carefully crafted television advertisements targeting undecided voters? The problem is that Tamraz's buying of access is not compatible with a political system premised on the assumption that all citizens are political equals.

Tamraz was merely a sidebar in the story of the 1996 elections. Years later Republicans still contended that Clinton and Vice President Al Gore technically violated the law with their 1996 fund-raising schemes, but no one disputed that Clinton not only accepted $62 million in taxpayer campaign money on the condition that he limit his expenditures to that amount but he also personally supervised and participated in fund-raising for the Democratic National Committee of an additional $45 million, almost all from wealthy people, such as Roger Tamraz. Clinton and Gore's frantic attempts to raise money for the Democratic National Committee caused them to engage in a multitude of at least unseemly activities, including humiliating stunts like promising overnight stays in the Lincoln Bedroom as incentives to large donors. The Republicans were no less active in raising money from wealthy benefactors.

The large influx of money in American politics corrupts the system in many ways. First, it preselects the candidates who can run an effective campaign. Campaigning is now so expensive that only candidates who can appeal to monied interests or finance their own campaigns can even get a toehold in the process. For instance, a Democratic governor from a small southern state with a strong belief in international trade attracted large contributions from Wall Street early in 1992; otherwise, we probably would not remember the name William Jefferson Clinton. A more populist candidate might have had less success on Wall Street. And the Clinton administration has worked zealously to open up foreign capital markets to Wall Street participation. In fact, his main adviser in this field, Robert Rubin, then the treasury secretary, was one of those early Wall Street contributors. This, of course, does not add up to corruption; it is just how the system works. But it does mean that Robert Rubin and his colleagues had a lot more say in the 1992 presidential campaign than the rest of us.

Proving exactly how much large contributions influence the decisions that candidates make after they are elected is difficult. To believe that elected officials promote only the interests of their contributors would be unduly cynical. But to believe that successful candidates do not reflect the views of those most instrumental in their election would be equally naive. The smart money would agree with Roger Tamraz: such large contributions have some influence on what government does. Otherwise, some of the most crafty people in the United States are wasting their money.

Many Americans no longer feel that elections are worth the bother. Although the 1996 elections were the most expensive in history, less than half of the voting age population actually voted.[12] And it is important to remember that many of those who do not vote are exactly the people who would benefit from being able to exercise their social rights like the right to earn a living or to receive a first-rate public education. Do they fear that Mr. Tamraz and his ilk have effectively bought the democratic process?

The need for reform seems clear. But meaningful campaign-financing reform has several obstacles to overcome. One is that campaign-financing reform raises extremely complex issues. Still, several reasonable approaches are available to Congress. However, both major parties (and especially the Republicans) are hostile to any meaningful reform of the system, which favors the interests currently in power. Republicans see little need to change. But instead of giving up hope that campaign financing will ever be reformed, it is instructive to remember that reform efforts usually begin as minority causes and only later are adopted by the major parties. For a hundred years the major parties refused to consider civil rights reforms. Civil rights groups mounted a vigorous attack on segregation decades before they convinced the Supreme Court that state-enforced segregation was unconstitutional.

Another obstacle, a 1976 Supreme Court opinion, is of special concern. It claims that meaningful reform is unconstitutional because it would violate the free speech rights of large spenders. This is similar to the Supreme Court's saying that not only is segregation permitted by the Constitution but it is required.

The case is *Buckley v. Valeo*.[13] It involved campaign-financing reforms passed by Congress in 1974 in response to public revulsion over the Watergate scandals. The legislation's goal was to prevent just the sort of attempt to buy influence that tarnished the Clinton-Gore campaign in 1996. The legislation was based on the belief that campaigns had become too expensive. One consequence was to make politicians overly dependent on the financial contributions of corporations and wealthy individuals; this led at least to a devaluation of the small contributions of average Americans and at most to corruption of officials through large contributions that functioned as bribes. Accordingly, the act set limits both on the amount of contributions that donors could make to campaigns and on the amount that candidates spend and that other groups could spend on their behalf. The legislation also provided for the public financing of presidential elections.

The Supreme Court ruled that the contribution limits and the public financing provisions were constitutional but that limiting expenditures by candidates or others violated their freedom of speech. This invalidation of expenditure limits presents a roadblock to reform.

The reasoning of the *Buckley* opinion is flawed in two major ways. The distinction between permissible contribution limits and impermissible expenditure limits just does not work in practice. Buying an expensive ad that benefits a candidate can provide the buyer with just as much influence as making a contribution in the same amount to the candidate's campaign. In fact, the direct contribution might be more beneficial because the ad gives the appearance of having been paid for by an independent party. For instance, the famous "Willie Horton" ads that played a major role in George Bush's election to the presidency in 1988 actually were not placed by the Bush campaign but by a supposedly independent group that favored Bush. Are we to believe that Bush was any less grateful because of the form of the support? Moreover, a contribution limit without a corresponding expenditure limit can never attain the goal of removing the influence of big money in politics. So long as rich candidates can spend without limitation, other candidates will just have to be more creative in finding the contributions necessary to match those expenditures.

The 1994 Senate campaign in California is a case in point. The race was between the multimillionaire Republican Michael Huffington and the Democrat Dianne Feinstein. Under the campaign law as truncated by the *Buckley* decision, a Feinstein supporter could contribute only $1,000 to her campaign. Huffington, on the other hand, could spend millions of dollars from his own pocket because these would be expenditures, not contributions. In fact, Huffington, who many felt had no strong qualifications for office other than wealth, actually spent $30 million, almost all his own money, on the election.

Nonetheless, Feinstein won the election, albeit by a slim margin. To do this she too raised huge amounts of money, mostly from wealthy people giving under a variety of legal mechanisms. Pros like Feinstein will always find a way to find the money they need to wage a winning campaign. Consider again the creativity of Bill Clinton and Al Gore. The real losers are the small contributors whose contributions were made virtually meaningless.

But the worst part of *Buckley v. Valeo* is not its unworkable distinction between permissible limits on contributions and unconstitutional limits on expenditures. The worst part of *Buckley* is its cavalier dismissal of the statute's goal of furthering political equality between citizens. Most of the Court's discussion of the statute assumed that the goal of the act was the narrow one of preventing bribery of federal officials, but that was not the statute's only professed goal. The other goal was to equalize the relative ability of all voters to affect the outcome of elections. Here is the *Buckley* opinion's discussion of the relevance of this goal: "It is argued, however, that the ancillary governmental interest in equalizing the relative ability of individuals and groups to influence the outcome of elections serves to justify [this expenditure limitation]. But the concept that government may restrict the speech of some elements of our society in order to enhance the relative voice of others is wholly foreign to the First Amendment."[14] With this opinion the Court found that the goal of fostering political equality is not merely outweighed by free speech concerns but is antithetical to the goals of the First Amendment. Any attempt to reform a system whereby the rich can use their wealth to dominate elections violates the purpose of the First Amendment.

This strikes me as the low point in modern American constitutional law. It belies a misunderstanding of the basic concept of a democracy. Here is how the legal philosopher Ronald Dworkin makes the point: "[E]ach citizen must have a fair and reasonably equal opportunity not only to hear the views of others as these are published or broadcast, but to command attention for her own views either as a candidate for office or as a member of a politically active group committed to some program or conviction. No citizen is entitled to demand that others find his opinions persuasive or even worthy of attention. *But each citizen is entitled to compete for that attention, and to have a chance at persuasion on fair terms,* a chance that is now denied almost everyone without great wealth or access to it."[15] This is the right to a voice that is heard. It is premised on the conviction that the essence of democracy is its commitment to the principle that citizens should participate as equals in their governance. To the extent that great wealth allows some citizens the ability to dominate the discussion, government may, indeed must, act.[16]

The goal of remedying the distortion of democratic debate caused by large infusions of money by wealthy people like Roger Tamraz is not only a permissible government goal but a necessary one if Americans are to be mindful of Brandeis's warning that "greatest menace to freedom is an inert people." Recognition of this point completely changes the constitutional balance in *Buckley*. Limits on expenditures do limit speech. Some reformers have argued that spending is not "speech," but that is not true. Because spending is speech and therefore has the potential to distort the democratic process, it must be regulated. Assume for a moment that the biggest contribution most Americans could afford for a presidential campaign is $100. Also assume that $100 can purchase one minute of "voice" in the campaign debate. That means that Roger Tamraz's $300,000 can purchase fifty hours of voice, while the average citizen gets only one minute, if that. Tamraz's voice is magnified by a factor of three thousand. To limit Tamraz to a contribution or expenditure of $1,000 clearly reduces his ability to speak, but it does not render him mute. A limit of $1,000 would still give him influence well beyond that of 95 percent of Americans. Reaching a perfect balance on this question is impossible. But a partial incursion on speech—limiting the amount a Tamraz may contribute—clearly furthers the goal of ensuring that all citizens have a realistic chance to be heard. Americans either have to allow Roger Tamraz to multiply his political influence by a factor of three thousand or place limits on him. If the United States is a democracy and not a plutocracy, the choice is clear.

Overruling *Buckley* is essential to instituting reform, but it is not enough. The history of campaign-financing reform has shown that so long as politicians need money to run successful campaigns and wealthy contributors believe that supplying that money is a good investment, they will find a way to make the necessary transfer of funds. For instance, tight limits on individual contributions spawned the creation of political action committees to efficiently funnel the same money to candidates favored by the PACs. Efforts to limit "hard money" contributions to candidates led to the concept of "soft money," contributions nominally given to the candidate's party for "grassroots" activities but functionally part of the candidate's campaign. A limit on soft money contributions to campaigns sparks the political ingenuity that funnels the same money into supposedly independent ads favoring one candidate. Ban "independent" ads favoring a candidate and someone will place eerily similar "educational" ads in their stead.

The constitutional goal is easy enough to state: politics should be, in Brandeis's words, a deliberative process in which all citizens can participate. Yet in the real world implementing the goal of a voice that is heard is very difficult because money so quickly tilts the process away from democratic ideals.

The only effective solution is to insulate the candidates from this insidious influence and require public financing of elections. Some have ridiculed public financing, calling it welfare for politicians. But public financing of elections turns out to be a sound public investment. Think first of the benefits. Under the current system public officials spend as much as half of their working hours raising money for the next election. President Clinton, for instance, spent hundreds of hours standing in reception lines shaking hands with potential donors, hours that he could have spent working for the public good. Second, publicly financed campaigns would attract a better class of candidate. The 1990s saw the early retirement of many successful politicians, each explaining that the burden of raising money twelve months a year every year had made public office more of a chore than an honor. Finally, it would also save money. Too often taxpayers foot the bill for the favors with which legislators pay back wealthy donors. The savings and loan scandal of the 1980s, which has cost taxpayers hundreds of billions of dollars, would never have happened if politicians from both parties had not been so dependent on contributions from the savings and loan industry.

In fact, the cost of publicly funded elections turns out not to be so costly after all. Sen. Mitch McConnell, a Kentucky Republican who is a rabid opponent of reform, claimed that the campaign costs of the 1996 presidential election came out to $3.89 for each eligible voter. He was trying to show that campaigns are not so expensive after all. But McConnell concedes that taxpayer financing of the campaign would have cost only $4 per eligible voter. That sounds like a bargain.

Maine voters have approved a campaign-financing plan that might serve as a model for reform.[17] It attempts to make an end run around *Buckley v. Valeo* by relying on public funding of elections combined with limits on voluntary contributions and spending. It provides public funding for all candidates who are able to demonstrate strong citizen support. It grants each eligible candidate a percentage of the average amount of money spent in previous elections. Because acceptance of public funding must be voluntary, a candidate still could finance a campaign by relying totally on the private funds of his or her allies. If such a candidate were to badly outspend her opposition, the Maine plan provides for the candidate receiving public funds to make an extra draw. The Maine reforms were implemented for the first time in the 2000 elections for the state legislature. The reforms appear to have been successful in realizing their goals of encouraging a broader spectrum of candidates to run for office and reducing the importance of raising money in running a successful campaign.

Neither the Maine reforms nor any variant thereof will yield a system that gives all citizens an equal voice. Wealthy people like Roger Tamraz will still be able to afford to work for a candidate without pay, a speech privilege most Americans cannot afford to exercise. But the abstract ideal should not be the enemy of practical reform; limiting the influence of big money is a good start on achieving that democratic process Brandeis pictured, one in which the "deliberative forces prevail over the arbitrary."

A Vote That Counts

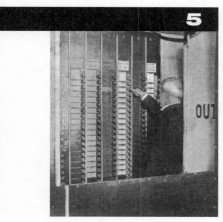

> [E]ach and every citizen has an inalienable right to full and effective participation in the political processes.
>
> —Chief Justice Earl Warren in
> *Reynolds v. Sims*

Recording a vote by pressing a knob.
Courtesy of North Wind Picture Archives.

The right to vote is central to citizenship. That is why it seems odd that it was not one of the "fundamental rights" of citizenship intended by drafters of the Fourteenth Amendment. But granting political power, not only to former slaves but also to women, was more than the reigning political consensus could accept. But if the term *privileges* of national citizenship were taken to be a dynamic term, the right to vote clearly would head the list of the privileges of citizenship today. It is axiomatic in a democracy that adult citizens have the right to vote. But I would argue that American citizens have more than a technical right to cast a ballot; I believe that every citizen must have a vote that counts.

Americans were shocked to discover in the 2000 presidential election that sometimes not all votes are counted. But the problem is larger than the use of antiquated voting machines. Even when all the votes are counted, not all votes matter. Experts consider a political campaign competitive only if the losing candidate receives at least 45 percent of the vote; they reason that if the candidates are separated by only a few points, the outcome is determined by the quality of the campaign run by each candidate. But if the winner receives more than 55 percent of the vote, the seat probably was safe from the outset and the campaign merely a ritual leading to a predetermined result. Using this yardstick of competitiveness, 201 of the 211 seats in the New York State Assembly elections in 1996 were noncompetitive, a result the *New York Times* attributed to gerrymandering by the major parties. The New York experience is the rule, not the exception; experts say as many as four out of every five elections involve safe seats. Therefore, in this very important sense, 80 percent of Americans are not casting votes that count—votes that have any chance of affecting the outcome. Maybe this explains in part the shocking statistic that less than half the eligible voters actually vote.

To some extent this dramatically undemocratic situation is caused by a phenomenon I discussed in chapter 4—the inequality in the ability of candidates to raise sufficient funds to run competitive campaigns. But the pervasive influence of gerrymandering in American politics also plays a role. Gerrymandering—the intentional manipulation of electoral districts to favor one candidate—has permitted the two major parties to create safe seats for their candidates.

My discussion of a vote that counts requires some review of a long history of American politics in which eras of political chicanery and reform alternate. Consider the political structure of a fictitious state called Midlandia in 1910. Say it had a population of one million, 200,000 of whom lived in the largest city, Metroville. If the lower house of its state legislature had ten seats, the districts for assembly elections might have looked very much like figure 1: eight single-member districts, each with a population of about 100,000 people, and one multimember district in Metroville where 200,000 people elected two at-large members of the assembly.

Figure 2 pictures Midlandia as it might have looked in 1960. More and more rural people had moved to the big city, which now had 520,000 inhabitants. But although the people moved, the assembly districts stayed the same. Midlandia still had eight rural districts, but each represented only about sixty thousand residents and the two at-large members from Metroville now represented 520,000 people. As a result, the rural interests, 48 percent of the state's residents, had 80 percent of the votes, ensuring that the legislature would adopt their policies. The residents of Metroville did not have a vote that counts.

Midlandia is an oversimplified but essentially accurate reflection

100,000	100,000	100,000
100,000	200,000 (2)	100,000
100,000	100,000	100,000

Figure 1. State Assembly Districts for Midlandia, 1910 (population: 1,000,000). The perfectly rectangular state of Midlandia, whose the population was perfectly distributed, had eight rural single-member assembly districts of 100,000 population each and one metropolitan district of 200,000 people represented by two at-large assembly members.

60,000	60,000	60,000
60,000	520,000 (2)	60,000
60,000	60,000	60,000

Figure 2. State Assembly Districts for Midlandia, 1960 (population: 1,000,000). In 1960 Midlandia was still perfectly rectangular but its population was no longer perfectly distributed. Its eight rural single-member assembly districts had only 60,000 residents, whereas the 520,000 people living in Metroville were represented by only two at-large assembly members.

of the situation in most states in 1960. And because the rural interests in control were not about to change the status quo, the problem ended up before the Supreme Court. The Court decided to act in the famous 1964 case of *Reynolds v. Sims*.[1] The Court stated that the equal protection clause of the Fourteenth Amendment requires that each assembly member represent equal numbers of citizens—or as the phrase goes, "one person, one vote." That ruling would have forced Midlandia to redraw its assembly lines (see figure 3).

In 1966 Metroville had five single-member state assembly districts, each with about 104,000 people, and the rest of the state was divided into five rural single-member districts of 96,000 residents apiece. It is easy to see the enormous transformation in power from the rural to urban and suburban interests mandated by the *Reynolds* decision. Many thought "one person, one vote" would work a quiet democratic revolution in American politics. This never came to pass.

Reynolds was premised on the principle that each citizen has a

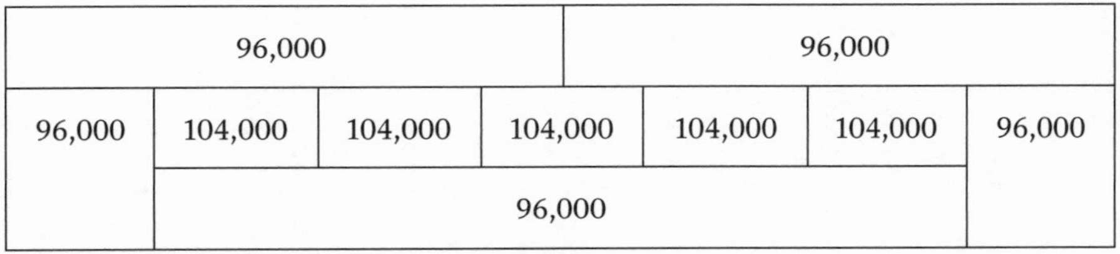

96,000

96,000

96,000

104,000 | 104,000 | 104,000 | 104,000 | 104,000

96,000

96,000

Figure 3. State Assembly Districts for Midlandia, 1966 (population: 1,000,000). The perfectly rectangular state of Midlandia had to redraw its assembly districts to comply with the ruling in *Reynolds v. Sims* (1964). In 1966 it had five rural single-member assembly districts, each with a population of 96,000, and five urban single-member districts of 104,000 residents each.

right to "full and effective participation in the political process"—
what I call a vote that counts. Most likely, the Supreme Court believed
that the "one person, one vote" rule would achieve exactly that when
it decided the *Reynolds* case. But the Court underestimated the creativity of U.S. politicians, who quickly found ways to draw districts with
equal populations (thus fulfilling the requirement of one person, one
vote) and still achieve narrow partisan goals. In other words, a system
that achieved one person, one vote still might not guarantee a vote
that counts in the sense of wielding effective political power.

To illustrate this point let us take a closer look at what might have
happened in Metroville, the capital of Midlandia. The legislature was
going to redraw the assembly districts for the 1980 elections. Assume
that Metroville still had 520,000 voters and five seats in the state assembly, and its population remained evenly dispersed geographical-
ly. Sixty percent of the voters were Democrats who lived in the valley in the southern part of town; 40 percent were Republicans who
lived in the hills in the northern part of town. How would the legislature draw Metroville's districts? Well, it had three choices. First, it
could have created a five-member at-large district in which all five
seats would be voted on by all Metroville voters. Or the legislature
could have redrawn the lines for the five single-member districts,
using vertical lines from north to south, as shown in figure 4. Or the
legislature could have drawn five single-member districts using hor-
izontal lines from east to west, as shown in figure 5.

Which plan would the legislature have chosen? Well, that would
have depended on which party controlled the redistricting process.
If the Republicans were in power, they would have chosen the east-
west plan in figure 5 because it would have given them majorities in

Republican 40%	Republican 40%	Republican 40%	Republican 40%	Republican 40%
Democratic 60%	Democratic 60%	Democratic 60%	Democratic 60%	Democratic 60%
District 1	District 2	District 3	District 4	District 5

Figure 4. State Assembly Districts for Metroville, 1980, North-South Redistricting (population: 520,000). This redistricting would have provided five single-member seats and made it likely that Democrats would win all five seats.

District 5	Republican 100% Democratic 0%
District 4	Republican 100% Democratic 0%
District 3	Republican 40% Democratic 60%
District 2	Republican 0% Democratic 100%
District 1	Republican 0% Democratic 100%

Figure 5. State Assembly Districts for Metroville, 1980, East-West Redistricting (population: 520,000). This redistricting would have provided five single-member seats and guaranteed that Republicans would win two seats and Democrats would win three seats.

two of the five districts, ensuring they would hold two of the five seats, a number roughly proportionate to their percentage of the city-wide electorate. If the Democrats were in power, they would have opted for either an at-large plan or the north-south plan in figure 4 because they would have been able to submerge the Republican voters in districts where Democrats held a 60-40 majority, quite possibly ensuring Democrats would occupy all five Metroville seats.

All this comes under the heading of gerrymandering. Note that under the at-large and north-south plans, the Republican voters might well have claimed they had been deprived of "full and effective participation in the political process"—a vote that counts. Their candidates usually would lose, and the Democrats would have had little incentive to pay attention to Republican views on policy. Note too that all the plans meet the requirements of one person, one vote as set out in *Reynolds v. Sims*. It was all perfectly legal.

Gerrymanders are the Achilles' heel of American electoral politics. Clever politicians armed with computers and census maps have the ability to gerrymander despite *Reynolds*.

To make matters worse, the Supreme Court never was willing to effectively confront the evil of gerrymandering.[2] But then impetus for reform came from an unexpected source. Angered by the Supreme Court's decision in *Mobile v. Bolden* (see chapter 1), which found that Mobile's election system was constitutional although it deprived minority voters of any representation, Congress took action to prevent some gerrymanders.[3] In 1982 Congress amended the Voting Rights Act to effectively overrule *Mobile v. Bolden*. Under the amended law, if a racial minority could show three factors were present in an existing at-large system, it could ask a court to order the institution of a new system of single-member districts, which would allow the minority to elect a candidate of that group's choice. The minority had to show that the majority did not vote for candidates favored by the minority, that the minority as a group did vote for the same candidate, and that the housing patterns of the minority would allow its members to prevail in a single-district election format.[4]

In hundreds of at-large districts African Americans and members of other minority groups were able to meet the requirements. Usually, it was easy to show that the majority and minority vote for different candidates, thereby fulfilling the first two requirements; the third requirement was readily fulfilled wherever racially segregated housing patterns existed, and that was almost everywhere. If minority groups convinced a federal judge that all three requirements were present, the court ordered new single-member districts to replace the old at-large elections that had effectively disenfranchised minorities. Figure 6 shows how the creation of three single-member districts in a city like Mobile would allow African Americans to elect an African-American candidate in one district. For the first time African Americans held political power roughly proportionate to their population in the city. They had a vote that counted.

During the 1980s and early 1990s federal courts all over the United States ordered political restructuring pursuant to the 1982 amendments. When the states themselves started to redraw districts after the 1990 Census, they also chose systems that created "majority-minority" districts (i.e., a racial minority that has a majority of the voters) in order to avoid being sued under the 1982 amendments to the Voting Rights Act. You could say that the Voting Rights Amend-

District 3	White 70% African American 30%
District 2	White 30% African American 70%
District 1	White 70% African American 30%

Figure 6. City Commission Districts for City Such as Mobile, Alabama, 1986. Each rectangle represents a city commission district in a city like Mobile, Alabama, after the 1982 amendments to the Voting Rights Act of 1965. For the first time African Americans would be able to elect at least one member of the three-member commission.

ments of 1982 in effect outlawed some gerrrymanders, those aimed at racial minorities.[5]

But the story did not end with the 1982 amendments to the Voting Rights Act. The Supreme Court got back into the act, ruling in 1993 that the new districts created to ensure minority voting power were often themselves in violation of the equal protection clause.[6] I argue in the next chapter that the Court's decision in this case misinterprets the equal protection clause. For now it is important to recognize that even if the 1982 reforms were found to be constitutional, they would not guarantee all citizens a vote that counts. In fact, although the 1982 amendments were an improvement on *Mobile v. Bolden,* they did not provide effective political power to minorities. The 1982 amendments did result in the election of more minority candidates, but they failed to give minorities more political influence in a substantive sense—the ability to enact legislation favorable to their interests. Figures 7 and 8, for example, show a metropolitan area called Midville with a population of 400,000, including 80,000 African Americans who live in the downtown area. The African Americans in Midville vote almost 100 percent for Democratic candidates, and the white vote is split, 55 percent Republican and 45 percent Democratic.

Figure 7 shows how Midville might have been districted before the 1982 amendments to the Voting Rights Act, especially if the Democrats controlled the districting. The 80,000 African Americans were split among four districts, thereby giving each Democratic candidate an extra 20,000 votes. Combined with the 36,000 white Democratic votes, the African Americans' votes would have allowed each Democratic candidate to overcome the Republican majority among white voters and win the election, 56,000 to 44,000. The Democrats would

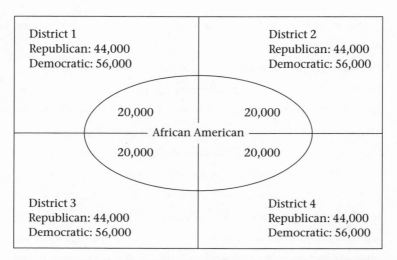

Figure 7. State Assembly Districts for Midville, 1980 (population of registered voters: 400,000). Midville had four single-member assembly districts, all of which would have been won by Democrats.

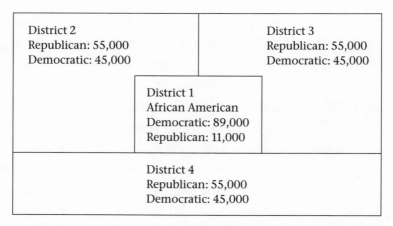

Figure 8. State Assembly Districts for Midville, 1988 (population of registered voters: 400,000). Midville had four single-member assembly districts of 100,000 voters each, three of which would have been won by Republicans, one by a Democrat.

have won all four seats and presumably favored policies more congenial to African Americans.

Figure 8 shows how Midville might be districted after the voting
rights amendments of 1982. This would have given the city a central
district in which African Americans constituted the majority of the
100,000 voters. They would have easily elected a Democratic candidate (89,000 to 11,000), probably an African American. So far so
good. But without those 80,000 Democratic votes from African
Americans, the Democratic candidates in the other three districts lost
to their Republican opponents, 55,000 to 45,000. So Midville was
represented by three Republicans and one Democrat, a legislative
delegation that, it is safe to say, was less supportive of policies supported by African Americans than the Democrats who were defeat-
ed. Simply put, experience has shown that while drawing "majority-
minority" districts helps minorities on a symbolic level, it usually
hurts them on a substantive level; more minority candidates may be
elected, but fewer laws favorable to minorities are passed.

The 1982 amendments resulted in a second problem. Although
most African Americans within the new majority-minority districts
now had a vote that counts, black Republicans in Midville found themselves submerged in a sea of Democratic votes. If one assumes that
most members of minority groups share the same political values, the
institution of "majority-minority" districts does give racial minorities
a vote that counts. But majority-minority districts don't solve the larger problem—that millions of Americans live in districts in which the
opposing party consistently makes up the majority. These citizens also
don't have a vote that counts. Unfortunately, this last group turns out
to be the vast majority of voters because legislators have tended to di-

vide up legislative districts into safe Democratic and safe Republican districts, thereby giving the incumbents job security purchased at the cost of effectively disenfranchising most citizens.

The history is worth reviewing. State legislatures, democratically representative early in the twentieth century, slowly became undemocratic because of demographic changes. The Supreme Court intervened in *Reynolds v. Sims* (1964) to insist that all states adopt a one person, one vote standard to ensure that all citizens were full participants in the electoral process. However, this reform was to a large extent neutralized by gerrymandering by both parties to favor their own candidates. Congress amended the Voting Rights Act in 1982 to combat one type of gerrymandering—districts drawn to submerge the voting power of racial minorities. The problem with the Voting Rights Act is that it gives relief only to racial minorities, ignoring other citizens.

A system does exist that would allow the votes of all citizens to count. Proportional representation (PR) is the election system that most modern democracies use. It avoids the problems of gerrymanders by not relying on geographic districts whose lines can be manipulated for partisan goals.

Here is how a PR system might work in a state legislative assembly with one hundred seats and four major parties: Democrats, Republicans, the Green Party, and the Taxpayers' Party. Each would field a slate of one hundred candidates. After the election, each would receive a number of seats proportional to its percentage of the statewide vote. Perhaps the Democrats received 35 percent; Republicans, 30 percent; the Green Party, 20 percent; and the Taxpayers' Party, 15 percent. Thus the Democrats would occupy 35 percent of the assembly seats; Republicans, 30 percent; the Green Party, 20 percent; and the Taxpayers' Party, 15 percent.

Every voter would have cast a vote that counts, for it resulted in the election of a candidate of the voter's choice. Under PR, no votes are wasted. The more votes the Green slate receives, the higher the Green percentage of the total vote, and the more Green candidates are elected. In the traditional U.S. system, if the Green Party candidate received 20 percent of the vote, the party would hold no seats in the legislature. But in proportional representation 20 percent of the vote translates into 20 percent of the seats. This would provide a strong incentive for people who share the Green ideology to vote. They can vote their principles and win.

The dynamics of the new legislature would also change under PR. Instead of the old system, which might result in a legislature made up of 55 percent Democrats and 45 percent Republicans, two new parties would be participating in the political process. For instance, the Democrats in this hypothetical situation would be forced to pay attention to the Green Party in order to enact legislation. The old system was weighted toward the views of that 10 or 20 percent of the electorate that politicians see as the swing voters. Under proportional representation the system has to pay attention to a wider range of views, Right as well as Left.

Proportional representation has seen various modifications in response to criticism. For instance, critics say that the traditional PR system does not allow voters to choose a candidate, only an ideology, because in the hypothetical situation I described earlier, the Green candidates elected will be the first twenty on the Green list even though these may not be the twenty most popular Green candidates.

Other critics point out that because the allocation is on a statewide basis, voters may be deprived of a local representative knowledgeable of local problems. Other critics charge that PR gives inordinate power to fringe parties, noting the experience in Israel, where small religious parties with as little as 1 percent of the vote have sometimes held the balance of power in the Knesset.

PR has evolved in response to those criticisms. For instance, in New Zealand the voters have adopted what is called multimember proportional representation (MMPR). Half the seats are allocated to geographic electoral districts where voters vote for a named candidate and the other half are allocated according to the percentage of the total vote received by each party. This form of PR attempts to keep some of the advantages of a local race with the ideological fairness of PR. New Zealanders have solved the problem of splinter parties by requiring a party to receive at least 5 percent of the total vote to qualify for any seats. In Germany the threshold for representation is 10 percent.

PR (or one of its variants) would be a giant move toward fulfilling the promise of *Reynolds v. Sims*. It would provide each citizen with an opportunity for "full and effective participation" in the political system. The 1982 amendments to the Voting Rights Act were in effect a partial PR system, requiring at least that racial minorities be provided a vote that counts.

Is PR consistent with the U.S. Constitution? That depends on the office in question. Certainly, it would not be applicable to the presidency. Nor would it seem applicable to the election of senators—the Seventeenth Amendment says they should be elected at large in the traditional manner. But Congress has the authority to control how members of the House of Representatives are elected, so it could prescribe some form of PR for elections to the House. And individual states could amend their constitutions to adopt PR for state elections. The major obstacle to the adoption of PR is really the opposition of the two major parties, which rightly fear the openness of proportional representation to third parties. In fact, voters need not wait for their legislatures to act; voters can amend most state constitutions by popular referendum.

I believe that adoption of proportional representation would materially advance the social rights program I have outlined in this book, especially if adoption of PR is coupled with the campaign-financing reforms discussed in chapter 4. The traditional system is heavily weighted in favor of a two-party system and the views of the swing voters who will decide an individual election. PR tends to encourage a multiparty system and the airing of views of less centrist groups. The two major parties today have little interest in social rights. PR would favor the creation of left-wing parties whose participation would be essential to governing coalitions. For instance, PR has made the Green Party in Germany part of the ruling coalition. This new power should also energize voters who would benefit from social rights like access to public jobs and good schools. The adoption of PR might lead to the electoral success of many of the reforms discussed in earlier chapters of this book.

But all this is speculation. PR could also result in the resurgence of nativist groups with a conservative ideology. Whatever the results, PR commands my support for the simple reason that it is more democratic. It allows more individual citizens the opportunity to participate effectively in the political system. That is all anyone can ask of a Constitution.

Equal Protection of the Laws

After Selma, ca. 1965. Courtesy of Tony Stone Images/Chicago Inc.

And when *this* happens . . . we will be able to speed up that day when *all* God's children, black men and white men, Jews and Gentiles, Protestants and Catholics, will be able to join hands and sing in the words of the old Negro spiritual "Free at last! Free at last! Thank God Almighty, we are free at last!"

—Martin Luther King

I pointed out in the introduction that section 1 of the Fourteenth Amendment contains three different clauses, each with a different task to perform. The privileges or immunities clause protects the basic rights of citizens, the due process clause insists on procedural regularity, and the equal protection clause forbids unjustified differences in treatment. My main concern has been how a new interpretation of the privileges or immunities clause can give the Constitution a more democratic cast, one more consistent with the basic moral premise of the Declaration of Independence. Therefore, technically, the equal protection clause is a topic beyond the scope of my discussion. Yet it seems essential to consider the role of the equal protection clause for several reasons.

First, many problems that courts have addressed maladroitly by reference to the equal protection clause can more fruitfully be discussed as privileges or immunities of U.S. citizenship. Because the Supreme Court until recently had completely ignored the privileges or immunities clause and has been reluctant to expand the scope of the due process clause, the Court has addressed almost all problems of civil, social, and political rights (except speech) as questions of equal protection, if it has addressed them at all. The right to vote and the right to an education are clear examples. Reclaiming the privileges or immunities clause would relieve the pressure to stretch the equal protection clause to meet all problems. It could then be used for its original purpose—helping to create an America where, in Martin Luther King's words, we are all "free at last" from the bondage of race.[1]

How does the equal protection clause complement the privileges or immunities clause? Many problems associated with race are in large part problems of class. Many "welfare children" come from minority families where the adults have a hard time earning a living, but even more children come from white families with the same problem. The good schools that will come from proper implementation of the privileges of U.S. citizenship will improve the lives of all American children, but because minority children disproportionately inhabit the poor districts like East St. Louis or Edgewood in San Antonio, they will experience a more dramatic benefit. But implementation of these privileges will not be enough; separate injuries are created by racial prejudice. Here the equal protection clause plays its special role.

So what should happen when policies inspired by the equal protection clause conflict with claims by white citizens regarding rights under the privileges or immunities clause? Answering this question requires discussion of the thorny topic of affirmative action.

But before I address the issues of contemporary concern, it is important to trace the history of the Supreme Court's interpretation of the equal protection clause. Like most constitutional phrases, "equal protection of the laws" is not self-defining. Since the equal protection clause was added to the Constitution in 1868, the Supreme Court has given the phrase many different meanings; some interpretations seem almost perversely hostile to the term's original intent.

The equal protection clause was passed, like the Fourteenth Amendment itself, primarily to aid the freed slaves. Southern states had enacted the Black Codes, which deprived the recently freed slaves of the legal capacity to own property or to make contracts or to exercise other civil rights. The equal protection clause was intended to forbid hostile legislation of this type.

The Supreme Court's first major interpretation of the equal protection clause came in 1880 in a case called *Strauder v. West Virginia,* which involved a statute that forbade African Americans from serving on juries. To its credit the Court quickly invalidated the statute. The Court was quite clear about the purpose of the equal protection clause: to grant to African Americans the "right to exemption from unfriendly legislation against them distinctively as colored."[2]

Unfortunately, the Court soon reversed course on the meaning of equal protection in the 1896 case of *Plessy v. Ferguson,* the case I discussed at the beginning of chapter 1. Briefly, the *Plessy* Court ruled that the equal protection clause did not forbid Louisiana from segregating railroad cars on the basis of race. The decision's import went well beyond railroad cars; it had the effect of legitimizing a whole system of racial segregation throughout the South—the American version of apartheid. After decades of political and legal struggle, African Americans convinced the Supreme Court to overrule *Plessy* in *Brown v. Board of Education* in 1954. The *Brown* decision, together with the actions of Martin Luther King and other participants in the civil rights movement, helped dismantle the state-enforced segregation of public facilities throughout the South.

However, *Brown* left unresolved important questions about what constituted racial discrimination. These questions were still unresolved as the 1970s began. Then, in two important decisions, the Supreme Court changed course once again, this time transforming the equal protection clause from a sword to be wielded by minorities into a shield for whites hurt by affirmative action programs.

The first case, *Washington v. Davis* (1976), involved a test used by the District of Columbia police in selecting recruits.[3] The police used a written test that African-American recruits failed at a much higher rate than their white competitors. The African Americans argued that using a test that was known to "deselect" them disproportionately was intentional and therefore constitutionally suspect. They did not claim that this made the use of the test unconstitutional, only that it required the police to justify the need to use the test. The police argued that because all recruits took the same test and the department had no proof that it had been chosen in order to harm African Americans, its racial effects were irrelevant and the department need not justify its use. Everyone agreed that intentional racial action was suspect; the disagreement was how to define *intentional*. The police argued that an act was intentional only if its intent was to have a certain effect on minorities; the minorities argued that the state intended all the knowable consequences of its acts.

The issue was crucial to the future of equal protection law. If the Court ruled for the minority recruits, the equal protection clause would require justification for the myriad situations in which a law has a disproportionate effect on minorities—when it hurts them much more often than whites. But if the Court accepted the narrow definition proposed by the police, the equal protection clause would become irrelevant except when the state explicitly admitted that its purpose was to disadvantage minorities or where proof of this same racist purpose could be presented. In the real world, however, no state ever admits to a racist purpose, and proving such a purpose in the absence of such an admission is difficult and expensive.

The Supreme Court in *Washington v. Davis* chose the narrow interpretation urged by the police: "[T]he invidious quality of a law claimed to be racially discriminatory must ultimately be traced to a racially discriminatory purpose."[4] The result has been that the equal protection clause has lost most of its value as a source of protection for minorities against "unfriendly legislation."

The Court's ruling was wrong on several counts. First, the normal use of the term *intentional* in U.S. law includes not only results that the actor desires but also those results that the actor believes or knows will occur or results that occur because the actor recklessly disregards the question of whether they are desired.[5] If I drive through a school zone at 100 miles per hour as school lets out, the law does not care whether I hoped to hit a child. If I do hit a child, the act is intentional. Second, the whole distinction between intentional and unintentional acts is especially unhelpful in the area of race because so much of racially motivated behavior is unconscious.[6] Finally, and most important, if the goal of the equal protection clause is to protect minorities from unfriendly legislation, courts should regard the legislation from the perspective of the minorities.[7] Unsuccessful black candidates for the police department in *Washington v. Davis* were much more interested in the effect the challenged test had on their career hopes than whether the decision to use the test was deliberately evil.

It is also important to remember that adopting the broad interpretation of *racial discrimination* does not invalidate any test or rule; it merely requires that the state offer adequate justification. If the test is a tool necessary for recruiting an efficient police force, it will be constitutional despite its effect on minorities. All the equal protection clause demands is a reasonable explanation of its necessity.

Washington v. Davis marked the end of the era when the equal protection clause played a major role in protecting minorities from unfriendly legislation. As I pointed out in chapter 1, in *McCleskey v. Kemp* (1987) the Court upheld a death penalty conviction in Georgia despite proof that African Americans were eight times more likely to be executed than whites; in the absence of proof that the procedures were adopted for a racial purpose, the justices allowed the execution to proceed. In chapters 1 and 5, I discussed the at-large election procedure that gave Mobile, Alabama, all-white municipal elected officials in the twentieth century and that the Court upheld because it had no proof that the system had been selected for the purpose of frustrating black political hopes.

But even as the Court shut down the equal protection clause as an avenue of relief for minorities, it found another use for it. It used the clause to strike down affirmative action legislation. In *Bakke v. Regents of the University of California* (1978), the Court confronted the issue of whether racial classifications used to help minorities faced the same presumption of unconstitutionality as those that harmed them.[8] The case involved the claim of a white applicant named Alan Bakke who said that an affirmative action program at the medical school at the University of California, Davis, had deprived him of equal protection. The program admitted minority candidates with academic credentials less impressive than Bakke's.

Justice Lewis Powell wrote the controlling opinion in the case. He made three different points. He ruled first on the preliminary issue of whether racial classifications that aid minorities are as suspect as those that harm them. In other words, does equal protection frown on legislation friendly to minorities as well as legislation unfriendly to them? Powell held that the same demanding standard applies to both types of classification.

I think Powell was wrong. A look at the reasons the Supreme Court is suspicious of racial classifications that harm minorities shows that these reasons do not apply to actions that aid minorities. For instance, the Supreme Court itself has said that the special protection for racial minorities is necessary because a minority constitutes a "discrete and insular" group that is unable to protect itself in the political marketplace.[9] Certainly, the white majority cannot claim to be such a powerless minority. It also is often said that racial classifications are suspect because they stigmatize the affected minority as somehow less worthy of respect. Segregation performed this stigmatizing function through laws that required that minorities not drink from water fountains used by whites, but I think it is nonsensical to argue that the white majority is stigmatizing a minority group as inferior in passing legislation that helps minorities. Finally, it is said that racial classifications are irrelevant to any proper government goal and therefore should be avoided. But that is not true if the government goal is to remedy past discrimination; if the discrimination was on a racial basis, race is the most relevant factor in formulating a remedy. The idea that the equal protection clause prohibits government from aiding racial minorities makes a farce of the main purpose of the Fourteenth Amendment, the improvement of the lives of the freed slaves so that they might live as independent citizens.

But that does not mean that a disappointed white medical applicant like Alan Bakke has no constitutional claim worthy of consideration. It merely means that his claim is not one based on the equal protection clause. His claim should be framed as a violation of the privileges or immunities clause, more precisely, the opportunity to earn a living or the right to an education, the very rights I discussed in chapters 2 and 3. Whether this claim would be successful is a difficult question, which I will address later in this chapter.

Having determined that affirmative action programs to aid minorities must pass the strictest of constitutional scrutiny, Powell then considered what state goals might be so compelling as to justify a racial classification. The California Board of Regents offered four different policy reasons for creating the affirmative action program: to increase the number of minority doctors because minorities were dramatically underrepresented in the medical profession; to counter the effects of "societal discrimination" against minorities; to increase the number of doctors who were likely to practice in areas of high minority population because minority communities were under-served by the medical profession; and to ensure that all students reap the "educational benefits that flow from an ethnically diverse student body."[10]

Powell rejected the first three goals as insufficient. His rejection of the goal of combating the effects of the societal discrimination against minorities was especially callous because that objective was the primary impulse behind the writing of the equal protection clause. For the Court to deny the validity of combating societal discrimination as a constitutional goal itself makes light of the whole constitutional enterprise. The goals of educating more minority doctors and producing more doctors who have connections with underserved minority communities are also completely in harmony with the goal of equal protection. Yet Powell ruled them all insufficient.

Powell then made a sudden detour from the direction in which his opinion appeared to be headed. He found that UC Davis could still use race as a factor in choosing its medical school class. Powell decided that the need to provide a "diverse student body" was a compelling government interest that justified certain forms of affirmative action, namely, a program in which race was one of many factors considered in accepting or rejecting an application. Powell in effect ruled that the right of minorities to freedom from discrimination is not compelling but that the need for white students to enjoy the educational benefits of an integrated educational environment is. Still, the key point to remember is that *Bakke* endorses the use of race for the purposes of affirmative action so long as the admissions procedures do not include a quota that automatically excludes consideration of the white applicant's merits.

The result of the Supreme Court's doctrinal coup in *Washington v. Davis* and *Bakke* was to rob the equal protection clause of its value as a judicial tool for protecting racial minorities from discrimination *and* to invalidate most efforts by legislatures to provide remedies for that same discrimination. The equal protection clause was no longer a shield for minorities but a sword for their opponents.

How would I change things? First, I would overrule *Washington v. Davis*. Courts would no longer limit the term *intentional* to situations in which they have proof that the action was purposeful in the sense of wanting to hurt minorities. The search for an evil purpose is wrongheaded in three ways. First, it gives an unnecessarily narrow definition to the term *intentional;* the usual legal assumption is that people intend the known consequences of their actions. If District of Columbia police officials choose a test that they know will disadvantage minority applicants, the result is not accidental. Second, the search for bad motivation is always costly and usually futile. People often do not understand the motivations behind their actions. And when they are conscious of their motivations, they often find they are conflicting. This problem of individual psychology is only multiplied when someone tries to determine the "purpose" of a legislature made up of hundreds of individuals. Most important, the search for bad motivation teaches the wrong lesson. It implies that, unless the court has evidence of a bad motivation, the consequences of actions are irrelevant. But the purpose of the Fourteenth Amendment was not to censure bad thoughts; it was to change the political status of the freed slaves. Toward this goal, motive is irrelevant; only consequences count.

Any legislation that the state knows will disproportionately harm minorities is presumptively discriminatory; accordingly, it must be justified. Such legislation must be examined closely to determine whether its harmful effect on minorities is necessary to the attainment of important state goals. Of course, this determination requires a balancing of the need for efficient government with society's duty to be fair to minorities, but this type of balancing is central to the mission of interpreting the Constitution. In chapter 4, I discussed the constitutional requirement to attempt to find some way to honor both a person's right to free speech and other government policies that may conflict with that right. Society owes the same duty to racial minorities—and must try to find some way to achieve important government goals like an efficient police force without using requirements that disadvantage racial minorities. This balancing approach is workable. Courts apply a similar approach in enforcing the provisions of Title VII of the Civil Rights Act of 1964 against employment discrimination. If an employment qualification has a disproportionate effect on minorities, it is not illegal per se, but it must be justified as necessary.[11]

This relatively small doctrinal change—focusing on effects, not purpose—would have an enormous effect on how courts consider government action that harms racial minorities. Consider, for instance, how a court applying this definition of *intentional* would approach the *McCleskey* case. In that case the Court had proof that prosecutors were much more likely to charge blacks accused of killing whites with the death penalty and juries were much more likely to vote for death in those cases. Under the broader interpretation of *intent,* this proof alone would compel the state to explain and justify the discriminatory effect of its laws.

Of course, a closer scrutiny of government action that disproportionately harms minorities will not always result in a ruling that the law is unconstitutional. Sometimes the disproportionate result will be justified. Perhaps Georgia will be able to show that the African-American defendants awarded the death penalty had committed more heinous crimes, such as mutilating as well as killing their victims. If so, the statistics would not show discrimination on the basis of race, only a permissible difference of treatment on the basis of the outrageous nature of the crime. Similarly, perhaps the police test contested in *Washington v. Davis* was necessary to ensure that all recruits had the reading skills necessary to be effective police officers in this era of bureaucracy. If so, the test is constitutional despite its effect on one minority group. The principle involved is a simple one. The equal protection clause does not require equal results for all races, but when government takes action that it knows will harm minorities, it should at least be able explain why the harm was unavoidable.

Overturning *Washington v. Davis* also would implicitly reject Powell's first two points in *Bakke*. Powell, relying on *Washington v. Davis*, assumed that unless minorities could show a racial purpose for enacting a law or administering a program, the white majority owed them nothing. Any additional "affirmative action" was completely voluntary and even then might be illegal as a violation of the equal protection rights of whites. But under the broader reading of *intent*, any law or practice that affects minorities disproportionately is presumptively discriminatory; it must be invalidated unless justified as necessary to some important goal. Determining whether a discriminatory practice is necessary involves asking whether the government goal can be achieved with less effect on minorities.

Consider the history of Metroville, a fictional city similar to most American cities in that it has a history of racial discrimination in the public sphere as well as the private sphere. It also has a history of racial discrimination in the awarding of city construction contracts. The population of Metroville is 50 percent minority, but less than 1 percent of the construction contracts have gone to minority contractors. Under *Washington v. Davis* those startling statistics would be of no constitutional consequence unless the complainant could prove purposeful racial discrimination. No action would be required of the city. Furthermore, if Metroville decided to institute "affirmative action" voluntarily, its program might well be found unconstitutional as a violation of the equal protection rights of white contractors.[12]

But under the broad definition of *intent,* a completely different situation arises. The damning statistics will be a wake-up call to Metroville, alerting it that it is vulnerable to a lawsuit by minority contractors. The disproportionate allocation of contracts makes the existing system presumptively unconstitutional. The city must either show that the disproportionate results are necessary or amend its practices to ameliorate the situation. The city will find it beneficial to study its bidding procedures to determine why minorities are losing out. The city probably will learn that the contracts are awarded through an "old boys' network" that excludes minorities and women. Because this procedure cannot be justified as necessary to the efficient operation of the city, it will have to institute affirmative steps to improve the situation. Some of this affirmative action need not be racial in nature. Perhaps the city could waive high bonding fees that are preventing small contractors, including many minorities, from

bidding on jobs. But other remedial action will have to use racial categories. For instance, if prior discrimination harmed the ability of
African-American plumbing contractors to make competitive bids,
the only sensible remedy will be one that takes into account the effects of the prior discrimination. No other type of remedy would fit
the injury.

Overturning *Washington v. Davis* changes the whole context in
which affirmative action programs operate. First, these programs are
no longer voluntary but presumptively required by the equal protection clause. Second, they need not any longer be geared to increas-
ing diversity for the benefit of whites but may be directed toward remedying the effects of discrimination on minorities. And when
Metroville finishes reforming its contracting procedures, it probably
will find it necessary to look at the percentage of minority officers on
its police force. If they are significantly underrepresented, rethinking
the recruitment process might make sense.

Is there any constitutional limit to Metroville's duty to restructure
its practices for awarding contracts to include more minorities? For
instance, why shouldn't the city require that 50 percent of all contracts be awarded to minorities? Or require that 100 percent of the
contracts be awarded to minorities for a period of ten years? The 50
percent quota would be an effective remedy for societal discrimination, the 100 percent quota even more effective. In fact, the reach of
affirmative action has two limits. The first is the number of qualified
minority contractors. Remedying discrimination is an important
goal for the city, but it does not outweigh the city's interest in safe,
well-constructed buildings. But even if Metroville had a sufficient
number of qualified minority contractors, at some point the affirma-

tive action policy runs up against the rights of qualified white contractors. The right involved, however, does not come from the equal protection clause but from the privileges or immunities clause. Every U.S. citizen has a right to the opportunity to earn a living. In chapter 2, I discussed this privilege of citizenship with regard to poor citizens who have a problem earning a living, but the right extends to all Americans.

The question then arises as how to reconcile these competing claims, each of which possesses a constitutional pedigree. Actually, the problem is really rather common in constitutional law. I discussed the same type of problem in chapter 4 when I considered the conflict between the rights of wealthy people to make large political contributions and the rights of all citizens to have a voice that is heard. But the frequency with which courts are called on to balance constitutional values does not make the exercise any easier or less controversial.

Luckily, the Supreme Court's own work in this area provides helpful insights. The case is *Johnson v. Transportation Agency, Santa Clara County* (1987).[13] I should point out that *Johnson* involved a slightly different issue than the one I am discussing; it involved a claim of sex discrimination and was decided under Title VII of the Civil Rights Act of 1964. But while there are important differences between race and sex discrimination, the structure of the doctrine in both areas is identical. And although Title VII and the Fourteenth Amendment are distinct legal texts, the reading of the equal protection clause that I advocate closely resembles the Title VII rule applied in *Johnson.*

The *Johnson* case involved an affirmative action program adopted by the Transportation Agency in Santa Clara County, California, for construction jobs. The plan had been devised after statistical studies showed a serious underrepresentation of women in skilled construction jobs. A job opened up for a road dispatcher, and several employees applied. Seven were deemed to possess the minimal qualifications and were interviewed by a panel that rated them numerically on traditional standards such as employment experience and seniority. The panel gave Paul Johnson, a man, the highest rating, a 75. Elaine Joyce, a woman, received the second-highest numerical rating, a 73. But the agency then decided, after considering all relevant factors, including the policy in favor of hiring more women for skilled positions, to award the job to Joyce. Johnson sued under Title VII.

The Court upheld the plan, saying that it was a reasonable effort to remedy the effects of past discrimination and it did not unnecessarily trammel the male employee's rights. The county could not have a quota that would automatically give the job to a woman, but gender was one of many factors that the agency could consider in making the decision. Had Joyce been given the job despite being found unqualified, Johnson would have prevailed. If his superiority on the traditional criteria had been more dramatic, he might have prevailed, but the two-point differential was not sufficient. The man had a right to compete for the job, and to have his qualifications considered, but his marginal edge in traditional qualifications did not give him a right to the job. This is the type of concrete balancing that courts have to engage in when whites claim that affirmative action policies violate their right to earn a living.

Powell made the same point in the third part of his *Bakke* opinion. Affirmative action programs should eschew quotas; they should make sure that the white candidate rejected has had her or his qualifications considered in comparison to those of the minority candidate accepted. But race can be a factor in the decision process. The balancing involved in affirmative action cases must always be specific to the context. Different facts will seem relevant in recruiting police officers, choosing a medical school class, and awarding city contracts, but the structure of the arguments will be quite similar. Both sides will tell their story, accentuating the equities of their position. The court will have to determine where the appropriate compromise of constitutional values lies. As in all lawsuits, the losing party will be disappointed.

But while the courts will have to use concrete facts in balancing the rights of the parties involved in each case, American society will have to accept an important constitutional principle. If Americans are ever to achieve the freedom of which Dr. King spoke so eloquently, the question must be not whether affirmative action is constitutionally permissible. It is mandatory. The question is how to devise forms of affirmative action that respect the rights of white citizens.

So the equal protection clause has a major role to play. Sometimes it supplements the role of the privileges or immunities clause, sometimes it endorses policies that may conflict with the mandate of the privileges or immunities clause. This tension between the two clauses should be expected in a document that promises both to protect minorities from discriminatory treatment and protect the fundamental rights of all citizens.

Conclusion   What It Means to Be an American

> Those who won our independence
> believed that the final end of the State
> was to make men free to develop their
> faculties.
>
> —Justice Louis Brandeis

I would like to end this book by considering a question that logically should have come at the beginning: What is the purpose of this book? One could say that it is a reading of the U.S. Constitution that accentuates the importance of the privileges or immunities clause of the Fourteenth Amendment. But I hope the reader will recognize that I have been discussing more than a novel reading of an almost forgotten phrase in the Constitution. The title of the book is actually a play on words; *Democracy's Constitution* is really an inquiry into what constitutes American democracy. What are the principles that distinguish the United States as a political and legal culture?

My answer, inspired by the Declaration of Independence, is that democracy requires the guarantee to all its citizens of a realistic op-portunity to pursue happiness as they define it. Toward this end, government must respect the fundamental rights of its citizens. Some of these fundamental rights are negative liberties (immunities) from government interference; others are positive rights (privileges) to government assistance. Some are protected primarily by the courts; others require action by Congress. They are all geared toward en-abling all citizens to achieve two goals: a realistic chance at financial independence in their private lives and a realistic opportunity to par-ticipate in the government of their public affairs. The term *democratic individualism* pretty well encapsulates the program I espouse. As Bran-deis pointed out, the goal of the state is the flowering of the individ-ual, but it must extend this opportunity to "develop their faculties" to all citizens.

I recognize that I have been engaged in a utopian enterprise here. In fact, as I discussed in chapter 1, my thinking is in direct opposition to current constitutional doctrine. But I hope that it is not utopian in the pejorative sense that it is wildly impracticable. The policies I advocate are not in any way impracticable in the sense that they are beyond the fiscal or administrative reach of the United States. Amer-icans could provide an excellent education for all children; doing so is just a question of finding the political will to allocate sufficient resources to the task.

But perhaps my argument is unrealistic because of today's cold political climate, and no one is likely to champion it. The arguments I have made would have looked much less unrealistic thirty years ago, when I first studied constitutional law. Maybe they will look more pragmatic thirty years from now. Predicting the future is difficult. My hunch is that the key is the fate of campaign-financing reform, which I discussed in chapter 4. The electoral process today is tilted heavily against democracy, making it exceedingly difficult for citizens without access to wealth to legislate reforms in substantive areas like jobs and education. Important people in both major parties have adopted campaign-financing reform in principle, so a chance still exists that this reform will eventually prevail and that more democratic campaigns might spark other reforms.

It would be naive to ignore the obstacles that confront implementation of the ideas I have outlined here, but cynicism is not an intelligent alternative to naïveté. I think the intelligent alternative is to practice what I call the virtue of "constitutional hope"—a faith that in the long run the American people will want a government that reflects their highest political ideals. It is in that spirit that I offer this book.

Amendment XIII

Section 1. Neither slavery nor involuntary servitude, except as a punishment for crime whereof the party shall have been duly convicted, shall exist within the United States, or any place subject to their jurisdiction.

Section 2. Congress shall have power to enforce this article by appropriate legislation.

Amendment XIV

Section 1. All persons born or naturalized in the United States, and subject to the jurisdiction thereof, are citizens of the United States and of the State wherein they reside. No State shall make or enforce any law which shall abridge the privileges or immunities of citizens of the United States; nor shall any State deprive any person of life, liberty, or property, without due process of law; nor deny to any person within its jurisdiction the equal protection of the laws.

Section 2. Representatives shall be apportioned among the several States according to their respective numbers, counting the whole number of persons in each State, excluding Indians not taxed. But when the right to vote at any election for the choice of electors for President and Vice President of the United States, Representatives in Congress, the executive and judicial officers of a State, or the members of the Legislature thereof, is denied to any of the male inhabitants of such State, being twenty-one years of age, and citizens of the United States, or in any way abridged, except for participation in rebellion, or other crime, the basis of representation therein shall be reduced in the proportion which the number of such male citizens shall bear to the whole number of male citizens twenty-one years of age in such State.

Section 3. No person shall be a Senator or Representative in Congress, or elector of President and Vice President, or hold any office, civil or military, under the United States, or under any State, who, having previously taken an oath, as a member of Congress, or as an officer of the United States, or as a member of any State legislature, or as an executive or judicial officer of any State, to support the Constitution of the United States, shall have engaged in insurrection or rebellion against the same, or given aid or comfort to the enemies thereof. But Congress may by a vote of two-thirds of each house, remove such disability.

Section 4. The validity of the public debt of the United States, authorized by law, including debts incurred for payment of pensions and bounties for services in suppressing insurrection or rebellion, shall not be questioned. But neither the Unites States nor any State shall assume or pay any debt or obligation incurred in aid of insurrection or rebellion against the United States, or any claim for loss of emancipation of any slave; but all such debts, obligations and claims shall be held illegal and void.

Section 5. The Congress shall have power to enforce, by appropriate legislation, the provisions of this article.

Amendment XV

Section 1. The right of citizens of the United States to vote shall not be denied or abridged by the United States or by any State on account of race, color, or previous condition of servitude.

Section 2. The Congress shall have power to enforce this article by appropriate legislation.

Notes

Preface

1. Professor Charles Black first pointed out the radical potential of the privileges or immunities clause. See Charles A. Black Jr., *A New Birth of Freedom: Human Rights, Named and Unnamed* (New York: Simon and Schuster, 1997).

Introduction

1. Garry Wills, *Lincoln at Gettysburg: The Words That Remade America* (New York: Simon and Schuster, 1992), 101.

2. See, generally, Robert J. Kaczorowski, "Revolutionary Constitutionalism in the Era of the Civil War and Reconstruction," *New York University Law Review* 61 (November 1986): 863.

3. *Slaughterhouse Cases,* 83 U.S. 36 (1873).

4. See *Saenz v. Roe,* 526 U.S. 489 (1999).

5. A good summary of the various contending positions can be found in John Harrison, "Reconstructing the Privileges or Immunities Clause," *Yale Law Journal* 101 (May 1992): 1385.

6. *Corfield v. Coryell,* 6 F. Cas. 546 at 551–52 (C.C.E.D. Pa. 1823) (No. 3230).

7. John Hart Ely, *Democracy and Distrust* (Cambridge, Mass.: Harvard University Press, 1980), 28.

8. William J. Brennan, "The Constitution of the United States: Contemporary Ratification," *South Texas Law Review* 25 (September 1986): 438.

9. See Taylor Branch, *Parting the Waters: America in the King Years, 1954–63* (New York: Simon and Schuster, 1988), 882–83.

Chapter 1: Too Important to Leave to Judges

1. *Plessy v. Ferguson*, 163 U.S. 537 (1896).
2. Ibid., 551.
3. Ibid.
4. *Brown v. Board of Education*, 349 U.S. 294 (1954).
5. The story is told in detail in Richard Kluger, *Simple Justice: The History of* Brown v. Board of Education *and Black America's Struggle for Equality* (New York: Harper, 1976).
6. *Dred Scott v. Sanford*, 60 U.S. (19 How.) 393 (1857).
7. *New York City Transit Authority v. Beazer*, 440 U.S. 568 (1979).
8. Ibid., 590.
9. Jonathan Kozol, *Savage Inequalities: Children in America's Schools* (New York: Crown, 1991), 23–29.
10. *San Antonio Independent School District v. Rodriguez*, 411 U.S. 1 (1973).
11. Ibid., 84.
12. See *Brown*, 347 U.S. at 493.
13. *Rodriguez*, 411 U.S. at 30.
14. Ibid., 50–51.
15. *Clark v. Community for Creative Non-violence*, 468 U.S. 288 (1984).
16. Ibid., 299.
17. *City of Mobile v. Bolden*, 446 U.S. 55 (1984).
18. *Reynolds v. Sims*, 377 U.S. 533, 561 (1964).
19. The facts related in this paragraph are findings of the federal district court in *Bolden v. City of Mobile*, 423 F. Supp. 384 (S.D. Ala. 1976).
20. The *Times* is quoted in Samuel Issacharoff, Pamela Karlen, and Richard Pildes, *The Law of Democracy: Legal Structure of the Political Process* (Westbury, N.Y.: Foundation Press, 1998), 719.
21. The Court formally recognized in *Davis v. Bandemer*, 478 U.S. 109 (1986), that gerrymanders to ensure safe seats could be unconstitutional but imposed on plaintiffs such a high burden of proof as to make successful challenges impossible.
22. *McCleskey v. Kemp*, 481 U.S. 279 (1987).
23. Ibid., 327.
24. Powell later expressed his regret at his vote in the case. See John C. Jeffries Jr., *Lewis F. Powell, Jr.: A Biography* (New York: Scribner, 1994), 451.
25. *McCleskey*, 481 U.S. at 315.
26. Ibid., 339.

Chapter 2: The Opportunity to Earn a Living

1. Eric Foner, *The Story of American Freedom* (New York: W. W. Norton, 1998), 10.
2. Quoted in Robert H. Wiebe, *The Opening of American Society* (New York: Alfred A. Knopf, 1984), 271.
3. Judith Sklar, *American Citizenship: The Quest for Inclusion* (Cambridge, Mass.: Harvard University Press, 1991), 64.
4. Ibid., 66–67.
5. Eric Foner, *Free Soil, Free Labor, Free Men* (New York: Oxford University Press, 1970), 16. Foner attributes the quote to "an Iowa Republican" and cites *The Debates of the Constitutional Convention of the State of Iowa*, vol. 1 (Davenport, Iowa: Luse, Lau, 1857), 193.
6. Lea S. Vandervelde, "The Labor Vision of the Thirteenth Amendment," *University of Pennsylvania Law Review* 138 (December 1989): 469.
7. Eric Foner, *Reconstruction, 1863–1877* (New York: Harper and Row, 1989), 243–47.
8. *Baldwin v. Fish and Game Comm. of Montana,* 436 U.S. 371, 386 (1978).
9. *Slaughterhouse Cases,* 83 U.S. 36 (1873).
10. Ibid., 113–14.
11. Ibid., 90.
12. See, for example, Laurence Tribe, *American Constitutional Law,* 2d ed. (Mineola, N.Y.: Foundation Press, 1988), 558–59; Philip B. Kurland, "The Privileges or Immunities Clause: 'Its Hour Come at Last?'" *Washington University Law Quarterly* (June 1972): 418–20; Charles Black Jr., *A New Birth of Freedom* (New York: Grossett/Putnam, 1997).
13. *Roe v. Saenz,* 525 U.S. 578 (1999).
14. *Allgeyer v. Louisiana,* 165 U.S. 578, 589 (1897), emphasis added.
15. *Lochner v. New York,* 198 U.S. 45 (1905).
16. *Meyer v. Nebraska,* 262 U.S. 390 (1923).
17. Ibid., 399, emphasis added.
18. *West Coast Hotel v. Parrish,* 300 U.S. 379 (1937).
19. See *Rankin v. McPherson,* 483 U.S. 378 (1987), in which the Court invalidated the firing of a county clerical employee on the ground that the termination violated the employee's free speech rights.
20. See *New York Times,* January 19, 2000, p. C6.
21. Paul Brest, "The Conscientious Legislator's Guide to Constitutional Interpretation," *Stanford Law Review* 27 (December 1975): 585.
22. See Steven J. Heyman, "The First Duty of Government: Protection, Liberty, and the Fourteenth Amendment," *Duke Law Journal* 41 (November 1991): 507.

23. *Goldberg v. Kelly,* 397 U.S. 254 (1970). See also Charles Reich, "The New Property," *Yale Law Journal* 73 (May 1964): 733.
24. Arthur M. Schlesinger Jr., *The Age of Roosevelt: The Coming of the New Deal* (New York: Houghton Mifflin, 1957), 286–88.
25. Frank Freidel, *Franklin Roosevelt: A Rendezvous with Destiny* (Boston: Little, Brown, 1990), 500.
26. See Mary Jo Bane and David T. Ellwood, *Welfare Realities* (Cambridge, Mass.: Harvard University Press, 1994), 143–62.
27. On the right to bear arms, see *U.S. v. Miller,* 307 U.S. 174 (1939).
28. See *New York Times,* June 27, 2000, p. A1.

Chapter 3: A First-Rate Education

1. *Meyer v. Nebraska,* 262 U.S. 390, 399 (1923), emphasis added.
2. *San Antonio v. Rodriguez,* 411 U.S. 1, 15 n.60 (1973).
3. *Pierce v. Society of Sisters,* 268 U.S. 510 (1925).
4. *Pierce,* 268 U.S. at 534–35.
5. *West Coast Hotel Co. v. Parrish,* 300 U.S. 379 (1937).
6. *Brown v. Bd. of Education,* 347 U.S. 483, 493 (1954).
7. See, for example, *Milliken v. Bradley,* 418 U.S. 717 (1974); *Pasadena Bd. of Education v. Spangler,* 427 U.S. 424 (1976).
8. *Brown,* 437 U.S. at 493.
9. Ibid., 493.
10. See, for example, *Robinson v. Cahill,* 62 N.J. 473, 303 (N.J. 1973); *Sheff v. O'Neil,* 678 A.2d 1267 (Conn. 1996).
11. See *New York Times,* January 5, 2000, p. A19.
12. I pointed out earlier in this chapter that the New Jersey Supreme Court, in *Robinson v. Cahill,* ordered the state legislature to reform its system of school financing. This does not mean that all New Jersey districts have an equal amount of money to spend. The affluent still have more, but the disparities are less.
13. See Mike Rose, *Possible Lives: The Promise of Public Education in America* (Boston: Houghton Mifflin, 1995), 428.
14. Lawrence W. Levine, *The Opening of the American Mind: Canons, Culture, and History* (Boston: Beacon, 1996), 92. Levine compared the lists of "classics" from two books edited by Norman Foerster. The first, published in 1916, includes nine "classic" writers; the second, published in 1963, listed eight authors of classics. Only Poe, Emerson, and Hawthorne made both lists.
15. *New York Times,* January 13, 2000, p. A18.

16. *Regents of the University of California v. Bakke,* 438 U.S. 265 (1978).

17. See James Crouse and Dale Trusheim, *The Case against the SAT* (Chicago: University of Chicago Press, 1985), 40–71, 89–132.

18. See *New York Times,* November 24, 1999, p. A1.

19. See *New York Times,* August 13, 1997, p. A16.

Chapter 4: A Voice That's Heard

1. See, generally, Michael Kent Curtis, *No State Shall Abridge: The Fourteenth Amendment and the Bill of Rights* (Durham, N.C.: Duke University Press, 1985).

2. See *Palko v. Connecticut,* 302 U.S. 319 (1937).

3. *Abrams v. U.S.,* 250 U.S. 616, 624 (1919), emphasis added.

4. See Laurence Tribe, *American Constitutional Law* (Mineola, N.Y.: Foundation Press, 1978), sec. 12-2.

5. *Clark v. Community for Creative Non-violence,* 468 U.S. 288 (1984).

6. *Whitney v. California,* 274 U.S. 357, 375 (1927) (Brandeis, J., concurring), emphasis added.

7. Robert M. Cover, "The Left, the Right, and the First Amendment," *Maryland Law Review* 40 (1981): 349.

8. *Whitney,* 274 U.S. at 375.

9. Philippa Strum, *Brandeis: Beyond Progressivism* (Lawrence: University Press of Kansas, 1993), 61–62.

10. *Whitney,* 274 U.S. at 375.

11. *New York Times,* September 19, 1997, p. A11.

12. See Charles Lewis, *The Buying of Congress* (New York: Avon, 1998), 9.

13. *Buckley v. Valeo,* 424 U.S. 1 (1976).

14. Ibid., 48–49.

15. Emphasis added. See Ronald Dworkin, "The Curse of American Politics," *New York Review of Books* 43, no. 16 (October 17, 1996): 23.

16. See Owen M. Fiss, "Free Speech and Social Structure," *Iowa Law Review* 71 (July 1986): 1405–25.

17. See, generally, Michael C. Campion, "The Maine Clean Election Act: The Future of Campaign Finance Reform," *Fordham Law Review* 66 (May 1998): 2391.

Chapter 5: A Vote That Counts

1. *Reynolds v. Sims,* 377 U.S. 583 (1964).

2. See *Davis v. Bandemer,* 478 U.S. 109 (1986), where the Supreme Court

ruled gerrymanders justiciable but imposed onerous burdens of proof on would-be plaintiffs.

3. *Mobile v. Bolden,* 446 U.S. 55 (1980).

4. See *Thornburgh v. Gingles,* 478 U.S. 30 (1986).

5. Gerrymanders are technically limited to intentional acts to skew voting strength; the 1982 amendments also made illegal unintentional districting practices that had the result of diluting a minority's voting strength.

6. See, for example, *Shaw v. Reno,* 509 U.S. 630 (1993).

Chapter 6: Equal Protection of the Laws

1. The equal protection clause, to be sure, applies to discrimination on bases other than race, but this chapter focuses only on the main historic role of the equal protection clause—to protect against racial discrimination. It also protects, among others, women and aliens. The protection of aliens would be especially important because the privileges or immunities clause is limited to protection of citizens.

2. *Strauder v. West Virginia,* 100 U.S. 303, 308 (1880).

3. *Washington v. Davis,* 426 U.S. 229 (1976).

4. Ibid., 240.

5. See American Law Institute, *Model Penal Code* (Philadelphia: American Law Institute, 1962), sec. 202.

6. See Charles Lawrence, "The Id, the Ego, and Equal Protection: Reckoning with Unconscious Racism," *Stanford Law Review* 39 (January 1987): 317.

7. See Alan Freeman, "Legitimizing Racial Discrimination through Racial Discrimination," *Minnesota Law Review* 62 (July 1978): 1049.

8. *Bakke v. Regents of the University of California,* 438 U.S. 265 (1978).

9. See *U.S. v. Carolene Products Co.* 304 U.S. 144, 152 n.4 (1938).

10. Ibid., 306.

11. See *Griggs v. Duke Power Co.,* 401 U.S. 424 (1971).

12. See *City of Richmond v. Croson,* 488 U.S. 469 (1989).

13. *Johnson v. Transportation Agency, Santa Clara County,* 480 U.S. 616 (1987).

Index

John Denvir is a professor at the University of San Francisco School of Law, where he teaches constitutional law and law and film. Earlier, he worked as a legal services attorney in California's Imperial Valley, where he represented farmworkers. He is the editor of *Legal Reelism: Movies as Legal Texts* (University of Illinois Press, 1996) and *Picturing Justice,* an online journal about law and popular culture (http://www.picturingjustice.com).

Composed in 9/16 ITC Stone Serif
with Helvetica Extended display
by Jim Proefrock
at the University of Illinois Press
Designed by Paula Newcomb
Manufactured by Thomson-Shore, Inc.

University of Illinois Press
1325 South Oak Street
Champaign, IL 61820-6903
www.press.uillinois.edu